"This book is simply genius. This is an amazing tool for church leaders trying to find their way through the convoluted maze of the online world. Every church leader needs this book in his/her toolbox."

—Tim Stevens
Executive Pastor at Granger Community Church
Author of *Pop Goes the Church*

"*#GoingSocial* provides a wealth of information about all forms of social media, giving pastors and others who want to influence culture the insights they need to do so. Digest this book, then engage your digital world."

—Ed Stetzer
President of Lifeway Research
Author of *Lost and Found* and *Comeback Churches*

"*#GoingSocial* is an invaluable resource for church leaders navigating the new frontier paved by these technologies and provides practical how-to steps to help churches and church leaders have a voice and get engaged in the conversation that's happening online."

—Tim Schraeder
Codirector of the Center for Church Communication

"A great resource to help you develop a social media strategy for yourself and your church."

—Josh Griffin
High School Pastor at Saddleback Church, Lake Forest, California

"Terrace Crawford knows how to leverage the power of connecting. His book *#GoingSocial* will transform your social networking into super networking."

—Tony Nolan
ealer

D1057798

"Terrace Crawford gives you an easy-to-understand overview of the social media landscape and how you can leverage social media in your ministry. The content is easy enough for everyone to understand but well beyond just basic knowledge. In individual chapters on Twitter, Facebook, YouTube, and blogs, you'll not just have an overall understanding of basic concepts but Terrace will also walk you through, step-by-step, how to get started. There are great tips and ideas, even for the most experienced social media aficionado. If you're intrigued by social media, you'll enjoy reading this book!"

—Todd Rhoades
Director of New Media and Technology Initiatives, Leadership Network and 100X

"This book will help you become fluent and effective in all things social media."

—Sam Luce
Nationally Recognized Christian Youth Speaker

"This book is real, relevant, and reliable! I'm thankful for how it will excel my ministry!"

—EJ Swanson
Nationally Recognized Christian Youth Speaker

"Church leaders tend to be lost in the maze of social media, and *#Going Social* makes it simple, relevant, and practical. My advice: read it, study it, and use it. It will make a difference in your ministry!"

—Dr. David Olshine
Director of Youth Ministry, Family, and Culture at Columbia International University
Founder of Youth Ministry Coaches

A Practical Guide on Social Media for Church Leaders

@TerraceCrawford

G o i n g S o c i a l

BEACON HILL PRESS
OF KANSAS CITY

Copyright 2012
by Terrace Crawford

ISBN 978-0-8341-2924-5

Printed in the United States of America

Cover Design and Internal Illustrations: Brett Kesinger
Internal Design: Sharon Page

Library of Congress Cataloging-in-Publication Data

Crawford, Terrace, 1977-
    Going social : a practical guide on social media for church leaders / Terrace Crawford.
        p.cm.
    Includes bibliographical references.
    ISBN 978-0-8341-2924-5 (pbk.)
    1. Social media—Religious aspects. I. Title.
    HM742.C73 2012
    254'.3—dc23

                                                                    2012024970

10 9 8 7 6 5 4 3 2 1

To my mother, Rita, and
to my Lord and Savior, Jesus Christ

CONTENTS

ACKNOWLEDGMENTS

I would like to thank the great folks at Beacon Hill Press and the Nazarene Publishing House—especially Chris Folmsbee—for allowing me to do this work. I would also like to thank God for stretching me through this project and allowing me to make so many friends along the way. I have appreciated each conversation and have valued each insight. Special thanks to my family (especially Rita, Jimmie, and Christina), friends (especially Nate Hogan, Seth Adams, Mike and Deb Glover, David Olshine, and Tony Nolan), ChurchLeaders.com, and Crossroads (especially my A-Team) for your prayers and constant encouragement. Thanks to Sean Cannell, not only for his friendship but also for contributing to the YouTube chapter. Thanks also to Bruce Nuffer and Rachel McPherson. I've enjoyed working with you. There are so many people I would love to name specifically, but I'm afraid I would leave someone out. If you've shared with me at all in this journey, whether through prayer, encouragement, or input, I am grateful for your contribution. To God be the glory!

Introduction
#More_than_Buzz

Cathy worked for a particular business to which I owed some money, and she was calling to discuss my account with me. I had been making regular payments to the company, but there was a period where there had been a lapse due to my unemployment. I thought I had been granted a forbearance for a specific period of time and when I thought I did not have to make payments, there were actually payments due. I had discussed this situation with prior customer service representatives from the company, but they could never offer any help with this matter. When representatives would call, they would ask about the lapse in payments and, after my explanation, would often offer to retro the forbearance period in order to clear me of the charges. They would simply explain that they needed me to complete a form and fax it to them and the matter would be resolved. Each time I would complete the form, fax it over, and then the representative would call me to explain that it wasn't possible for one reason or another.

Cathy called this particular day and asked about the lapse. I explained to her, as I had explained numerous times prior to her co-workers, the reason for the lapse. Within a brief moment Cathy said, "Well, Mr. Crawford, all you need to do is complete this form and fax it over to me and I'll get you clear of these charges."

Sigh.

"Mr. Crawford?"

I immediately chimed in, "This won't work, Cathy. I've completed your form numerous times but it hasn't worked.

"You haven't spoken with me before, have you?" Cathy replied.

"No, I haven't, but it won't work. It's a waste of my time."

Cathy replied, "You are such a man!"

Huh? That didn't sound very professional. "Excuse me?"

"Why are you so stubborn?" she asked.

I laughed.

"You know what? I'm done with you," said Cathy.

"Huh?" I replied. "Whoa, whoa, whoa, wait a minute!" Reverse psychology will get you every time.

"Mr. Crawford, I have other people to talk with on the phone who need my help. Are you going to let me help you?"

One more time I stated, "Cathy, it won't work."

"Terrace," she replied, "why do you have such defeat in your heart?"

Insert crickets. This was not an ordinary customer service representative. Why I didn't get that minutes earlier, I don't know.

"I don't know," I answered. I was shaken by her question.

"Terrace," she said, again calling me again by my first name, "let me help you."

"Ok," I replied. "I'll complete the form and fax it over."

The next day I spoke with Cathy again. "Mr. Crawford, everything has been taken care of and we've been able to clear you of those particular charges."

I was amazed. I thanked Cathy for her help and hung up the phone.

A few weeks later I was meeting a fellow youth worker friend, Nate Hogan, for lunch. I told him about the bizarre conversation and about the things God was doing in my heart, how he used that lady in my life. He said, "That's the craziest thing I have ever heard." Then he asked, "Have you called her back and told her what that call meant to you?"

"No, I haven't," I answered.

After leaving the lunch, I decided to call Cathy. I picked up the phone, started to dial the phone number, and then ended the call. I did this several times, each time talking myself out of calling because I knew the chances were slim to none that I would actually get her on the phone. Finally I dialed, wondering what the chances were that I would get Cathy on the phone when dozens of other representatives were taking calls. The phone rang and then I heard, "Hello, this is Cathy, how can I help you?"

"Cathy! You are just the person I wanted to speak with," I said.

"Well, hello there! Can I have your full name and your account number?"

"Oh, I'm not calling for business," I responded.

"Oh? You're calling for pleasure?"

I laughed and recounted the story to Cathy about the day I called. When I had finished, I thanked her.

"Cathy, I just want to say thank you. You have impacted my life through your words that day. God used you to speak to me."

Immediately I heard Cathy weeping on the other end of the phone. "Cathy?"

"I'm sorry," she said. "I sit here every day and take phone call after phone call, wondering if I am making a difference. I never hear back from anyone."

"Cathy, can I ask you a question?" I asked. "Are you a Christian?"

"Yes," she replied. "I'm sorry about crying on you. It's just that I literally prayed before you called today and told God that I could not do this anymore. That I could not take one more phone call. And then you called me to tell me this."

I asked, "Cathy, why did you ask me if I had defeat in my heart?"

"Terrace," she said, "I'm not supposed to share like this, but I won't be working here much longer. I have stage four cancer and the doctors say that it is only a matter of time before I die. I talk to people every day who have problems and I hear the hopelessness in their voices and I think to myself, 'If I can beat this, you can definitely beat that.'"

"Oh, Cathy, I'm so sorry," I continued. "God used you to speak into my life, and I will tell your story for years to come."

I ended the call that day astonished at how God worked through all of this. Unbelievable. Before we finished our conversation that day, Cathy told me about her blog online. Ever since then I've been reading along and I am happy to say that she is still with us. In fact, we're friends on Facebook! Her impact is great. In one of her latest blog entries, she stated how she is connecting with people on several different continents now through social media. I assume she's sharing that same hope she shared with me. You see, social media is about more than just buzz. Yes, buzz can be a byproduct, but social media can be a powerful tool that God can use in your life and in your ministry.

It's fascinating to think that Jesus Christ walked this earth two thousand years ago and people still talk about it. This one central message, the gospel, has transformed lives and continues as powerfully as when it first began. I'm convinced that if Jesus Christ walked the earth today that he would be using Facebook, Twitter, blogs, and YouTube to spread his message. The thing is, Jesus would not be using these social media platforms just for pure enjoyment. I think he would have one particular thing on his mind, and that would be connecting with people and changing lives.

I'll never forget the day I first heard about anything pertaining to social media. I was working for a radio station in Columbia, South Carolina, when the news director, Bob Holmes,[1] came to my desk and asked me, "Terrace, what is a blog?"

I had no clue.

He scratched his head and said, "I figured if anyone knew what a blog was, you'd be the one!" I later found out he said that because I was the "young" guy on the block.

That day I had no clue what a blog was and yet today I'm writing a book to help others understand media a little bit better. Ironic, no?

The evolution of media has been an interesting thing to watch. That was a long time ago, so what showed up that day in my Google search differs from what we would see today. "Social media," including blogging, is quickly changing (and may eventually replace) the traditional forms of media from years ago.

So what does social media have to do with you?

That is a question I will answer throughout this book. I enjoy using social media to help me with the work I do in ministry, and my goal is that you will come away from your reading with a greater sense of awareness (and maybe even appreciation) of the tools that are at our disposal today.

While this book may be considered a brief overview of the phenomenon of social media, it is also intended to help fill in a few of the gaps you may have and will hopefully serve as a reference or practical guide for you to get started.

Lost in #Translation

"Social media is actually not a very good name for the realm it is supposed to define. The issue I have is with the word 'media,' which is defined as a way to communicate information to large amounts of people. That calls to mind stacks of newspapers, blaring TVs, and babbling radios—just vast amounts of information flooding out no matter who is (or isn't!) listening. It is kind of like a shotgun blast, spewing out bits of information everywhere in the hopes that maybe one tiny piece will actually find its intended target."[2]

—Matt McKee

I'll never forget sitting in a classroom on the first day of school await-ing the arrival of my Spanish teacher. When she arrived, she shut the door, walked to the front of the room, and began speaking nothing but Spanish. She talked incessantly for what seemed like a full hour . . . in nothing but Spanish. I was completely lost! I looked around the room and wondered if anyone else thought this was ridiculous. Pretty soon I started to tune her out. Finally she returned to speaking English and we all applauded. OK, that last part didn't happen . . . but you get how happy I was that I wasn't lost anymore.

This may be the same sort of scenario you find yourself in when it comes to social media. There is an entire language being spoken and a world that exists that is unfamiliar to you, and maybe some things get lost in translation. I wish I could say that Spanish was the only subject matter that has been foreign to me over the years, but the truth is that it's not. We tend to shy away from things that we don't understand or that aren't familiar to us. Sometimes we even discredit these things for the same reasons. This book can help you understand the world of social media and how God might use it to help you have conversations with others. Isn't that alone enough of a reason to read on and em-brace the unfamiliar?

Let me put you at ease by saying that if you have not yet embraced social media, you are not alone. I've done social media seminars over the last couple of years and each time I ask the audience, "Who has a Facebook account?" or "Who uses Twitter?" and more often than not, there are many people who have never signed on. Despite that fact, they decided to show up to the seminar and learn. They did not want to be lost in translation any longer.

Not understanding social media is just one reason church leaders shy away. There are other reasons too. Let me share a few.

TOP FIVE REASONS PEOPLE DON'T USE SOCIAL MEDIA

THEY ARE UNFAMILIAR WITH IT. Even though there are millions of people that log on to a social networking site every day, there are just as many people who are not using these sites. One of the main reasons is that they are uncomfortable entering a world that is foreign to them.

THEY ARE AFRAID THEY'LL FEEL A LOSS OF CONTROL or lose the ability to manage things. It can be intimidating to post things about yourself on the Internet knowing the whole world can see them. I know a number of pastors who are afraid of developing a Facebook or Twitter page because they are afraid to share their lives with the public. And, yes, social media makes things public, but isn't communicating with others why we are in ministry?

THEY'RE TOO BUSY. I hear this all the time. "Social media seems like a complete waste of time." "Why do I need to tweet about what I'm eating? That's stupid!" For what it's worth, many Twitter users will agree they don't want to hear about every meal you have, but people do want to be a part of your life. Whether it's on Facebook, YouTube, blogs, or Twitter, you can make a difference by meeting people. Technology has made things pretty easy too. For instance, from my smartphone I can update my Twitter feed in a matter of seconds. If you really see the value in connecting with people, taking seconds to share something is totally worth it.

THEY'RE SCARED OF WHAT PEOPLE MAY SAY. Some people are worried others will misunderstand their posts and be offended, while others fear that they will receive nasty responses to their posts. It is certainly true that we must be exceptionally careful about our words when there is no verbal context for them. Sadly, I've heard of a number of people who have been let go from their positions because they mentioned inappropriate things on social networking platforms. Yet being careful with our words is one of the characteristics of a Christian anyway, regardless of where we use them.

TOO MUCH NOISE. Another popular reason some church leaders don't use social media is because they feel there is already too much "noise" in their lives. I can understand this one too. I have accounts on a variety of social networking platforms and it does get a bit noisy, but there are ways to turn the volume down. For instance, I have approximately twelve thousand people who currently follow me on Twitter. I also follow nearly half of them, and that can be a lot of noise. However, various web and mobile apps allow you to filter your tweets to reduce the noise. I can set up the app I use to read Twitter posts so that I only hear from certain people (close friends, colleagues, etc.), thus turning down the volume to a level I like.

After I discovered what a blog was, I immediately took the first step toward learning more—I started reading blogs. It was a wonderful experience. I looked for blogs that related to my interests. Even though I was working in radio at the time, I enjoyed ministry to youth and began to surf the Internet for youth ministry blogs. Sadly, in those days there weren't many. In fact, I can't recall finding *any*, but I did find a few others that I still enjoy, and it helped me get started.

If I hadn't decided to explore and learn a few things, I could have still been lost in translation all this time. I began reading more and more about blogging until eventually (it seemed almost overnight) ministry blogs were popping up all over. Every morning I would sit down and read each blog post—occasionally leaving comments and sometimes writing one myself. It became something I enjoyed. There was a sense of community about it. Suddenly I didn't feel "lost" anymore.

What Is
#socialmedia?

"It is difficult, indeed dangerous, to underestimate the huge changes this revolution will bring or the power of developing technologies to build and destroy not just companies but whole countries."

—Rupert Murdoch

Did you know that over 50 percent of the world's population is under thirty years old and that 96 percent of them have joined a social network? (Qualman 2012). Did you know that together Ashton Kutcher and Ellen Degeneres have more Twitter followers than the populations of Ireland, Norway, and Panama combined? Would you be surprised if I told you that Facebook added over two hundred million users in less than a year, and that if Facebook were a country it would be the world's third largest ahead of the United States of America and only behind China and India? (Qualman 2011). This is the reality of social media today.

So what is it? Social media simply enables a two-way conversation. While the word "social" may seem too casual to denote anything important, it merely pertains to the human need to connect or seek companionship from other people. Since the garden of Eden we've had a need to be around other human beings, and we are often drawn to like-minded people. It's God's design. We find it important (some of us more than others, of course) to also share our thoughts, ideas, and experiences with those people.

The word "media" pertains to the tools we use to communicate or make those connections with other people on the planet. There are many tools and technological platforms used to communicate: television, computer, mobile phones, text messaging, email, sharing photos, videos, and much, much more.

Social media has made communicating and connecting so much more effective than it was in the past. This is because it has empowered users to select information from sources they trust (organizations, companies, leaders) and allows for interaction (a two-way communication or "conversation") with those sources. Additionally, it taps into others in the community who have had interaction with the same source as you. For example, let's say you go online to book a hotel room. Before you book a room you can talk to a representative about what amenities are offered at that hotel and you can also read the reviews (shared experiences) of others who have stayed at that particular hotel. After your stay, you are encouraged to write a review of your experience at that hotel too. You can even share your review through social media networks (Facebook, Twitter, etc.). What is unique about this type of media is that your review has the potential of being read by hundreds of thousands of people, and therein lies social media's power.

Some time ago a ministry in another state asked me to speak. After the event host made my hotel reservation, the hotel sent an email with the information about my accommodations. Because I didn't recognize the name of the hotel, I went online to check it out. One of the very first reviews was pretty harsh. It read something like this: "The hotel was pretty dated and smelled smoky. We also were not happy to find out that we had to go across the street to another hotel to eat our free continental breakfast." Houston, we have a problem. Fortunately there were a few other reviews that were more positive. The website also had an option to chat with a representative. I asked about the amenities, including the free breakfast, and the employee informed me that what I had heard was true—I would have to go across the street to the Best Western for my breakfast. The reason? The on-site restaurant and lounge were temporarily under construction. Everything was beginning to make more sense and I was now prepared for what I would find when I arrived. I was most impressed by the staff's customer service and ended up writing a nice review of the hotel when I returned home. I was also able to share my experience via my social networks.

ROAD MAP FOR THE REST OF THE BOOK

Now that we've discussed a few basic forms of social media, I'd like to narrow the field a bit. I will focus on a few of the top social media platforms that church leaders are using today. I will share with you how to get started on Facebook, Twitter, blogs, and YouTube. I will also share a chapter on some platforms and networks that are popular but aren't as widely used in the church today. I will conclude with twenty examples of church leaders and ministries that are leveraging social media today. One important thing to note: the pace at which things change in Internet culture means the exact content of this book will likely be a little different by the time you read it. I would encourage you to visit my website at www.TerraceCrawford.com for the latest on what types of social media ministries are using effectively today, and how any of this information might have changed.

BASIC FORMS OF SOCIAL MEDIA

Social networks: Popular websites that allow people to set up personal pages and connect with friends and family in order to communicate and share content. The biggest social network is Facebook, followed by Myspace and Bebo.

Blogs: One of the best-known forms of social media today is blogs. These websites are like online diaries or journals.

Wikis: These websites allow people to add or edit content, acting as a communal document or database. The best-known wiki is Wikipedia, an online encyclopedia with over two million English-language articles. A number of experts have studied the accuracy of Wikipedia, and most agree that even though the general public can update the articles, they have a high degree of credibility.

Podcasts: Audio and video files that are available by subscription through services like Apple's iTunes. You can listen to sermons, interviews, music, and more by subscribing to various podcasts.

Forums: Areas for online discussion, often focusing on specific topics and interests. Forums were created before the modern social media movement and are a powerful and popular element of online communities.

Content communities: These communities organize and share particular kinds of content. The most popular content communities are formed around photo sites (like Flickr), bookmarked links (like Delicious), and video sites (like YouTube). But there are a multitude of these types of sites based on various hobbies and interests.

Microblogging: When bite-sized nuggets of information called "updates" are distributed through online and mobile phone networks. Microblog site users are encouraged to post updates to their accounts in one hundred forty characters or less. Twitter is the front-runner in this field.

3

Here Comes #theBoom!

"We don't have a choice on whether we DO social media, the question is how well we do it."

—Erik Qualman, "Social Media Revolution"

Most social media books focus on how to get your brand or product (in this case, your church or ministry) on the map. In fact, when I recently visited a few local bookstores to check out the section on social media I noticed that it was overrun by marketing books. Many social media veterans would argue, "Of course! That's what social media is about!" Here's the thing . . . that is not what all social media is about, and that is not what this book is about. You see, I use social media for networking. I love connecting with people and having conversations. I also love pointing leaders to resources they can use. I don't consider any of this "marketing."

While having an online presence can really help build your brand and put your ministry on the map, I would say that this benefit is a byproduct. First and foremost, social media should be used to connect with other people.

FIND OUT MORE ABOUT THE CITY IN THE LAST CHAPTER OF THIS BOOK.

I love what I read on The City blog recently. The City is a growing online social network hub and software company that helps churches. Joe Filbrun explains that technology is not the goal in one post: "The goal of The City isn't to get people to spend more time online. The goal of The City is to help pastors and leaders in local churches use the features we create to mobilize their people to live out the Gospel, so that the world can see the greatness of God as they encounter the love, grace, and truth of Jesus in the lives of His people" (Filbrun 2011).

THE DAY SOCIAL MEDIA SAVED MY LIFE

Social media has great power. I learned this firsthand one hot summer day in June of 2009 when I was traveling in Virginia. My car started to overheat as I approached a tunnel, and I immediately began praying that my car would not leave me stranded inside the tunnel. Fortunately I was able to get my car through the tunnel safely and eventually I was able to pull over safely on the shoulder. I immediately sent a tweet about the breakdown. If you don't follow me on Twitter (@terracecrawford), here's what you missed that day:

6:52 p.m.
My car broke down on a bridge. DOT just put out the road flares.

7:36 p.m.
This DOT lady towed me off the bridge tunnel and left me in this abandoned parking lot on the other side. Help!

7:42 p.m.
Oh no. I have to pee!

7:54 p.m.
Oh no! it's raining now!

9:13 p.m.
2.1 hours later. Vultures circling.

9:58 p.m.
Rusty & Tiffany Dailey came to my rescue! Thanks, guys! #coolpeople

Soon after I tweeted about my car trouble, I got a call from a friend to see if I needed help. Actually, I started getting replies on Facebook and texts to my mobile phone too. You see, you can sync platforms such as Twitter and Facebook so that when you make an update to one of them, it updates all of them. After I sent my first tweet on Twitter that day, it posted the tweet to Facebook as a status update. Within two hours or so I had numerous people calling to find out where I was and if I was OK. Pretty soon a mechanic arrived and repaired my car (at no charge, I might add) because he read my status through these social media platforms. This is one example of the power I'm talking about.

OK, you're probably asking, "How did social media save your life?" Well, I wasn't in danger, but at least I got your attention.

NEW FINDINGS:
HOW AMERICANS ARE USING SOCIAL MEDIA

Social media has really evolved . . . and quickly. There has been an explosion or "boom," and its effect is far-reaching. A few short months ago at a popular conference called "BlogWorld," Tom Webster (VP of Edison Research) released some preliminary data from his research group in cooperation with Arbitron. I shared these new findings on social media with some of my colleagues because I thought it was rather telling about how Americans are using technology today:

1. **Social media's reach:** More than 51 percent of Americans (ages twelve and up) are on one or more social media platform today. Over

forty-six million of those Americans use their social media platforms at least once daily (Webster 2011).

2. Demographics: The typical social media user is apparently a thirty-five-year-old Caucasian woman. Only 43 percent of men use social media. Other numbers: 64 percent of Caucasians use social media, versus 28 percent of African American and Hispanics combined. Only 8 percent of social media use is comprised of posts from other minorities.

3. Mobile users fueling growth: More than half of social media users are using their smartphones to update their accounts. In fact, 64 percent of those who use social media use their phones to update their statuses.

4. Twitter vs. Facebook: Eight percent of those recently surveyed say they use Twitter, while 51 percent of users said they had a Facebook profile. But don't count Twitter out . . . that 8 percent translates to over twenty million Americans.

5. Location-based services and apps: Only about one-third of social media users actually know what location-based services are. You know . . . Foursquare, GoWalla, and the like. Even though GoWalla is already defunct, the number of users of similar services is expected to grow exponentially over the next couple of years.

6. Broadband users: Six out of seven American homes have broadband Internet access, while nine out of ten are online. Wonder how many of those connect (or will connect) through social mediums over the next few years?

7. Brands on social media: Social media has really put brands on the map. Because of platforms like Facebook and Twitter, companies have made a ton of money. The question is, how will you leverage it? Recent research shows that one in four users are following a brand on social media.

THE GROWING PHENOMENON

There's no doubt that social media is a growing phenomenon. I'll never forget the day I heard that Queen Elizabeth had launched her own YouTube channel so that she could communicate with England. Do you remember how social media turned a grassroots campaign into one of the most successful presidential campaigns in history—the one that got Barack Obama elected president of the United States? People everywhere seemed to connect with Obama's message of "hope and change" and, regardless of what you think of him now or what political party you support, you have to recognize that he was speaking the language of the people and meeting them online. He was culturally relevant. Just after Barack Obama was elected as the forty-fourth president of the United States, he began asking if he could use his smartphone to respond to messages from the people.

The reach of social networking is unbelievable. This new revolution in technology has proved itself, especially in the aftermath of natural disasters. For the first time in the history of global tragedies, nearly forty-two million dollars was donated to the Red Cross using texts (Mollencamp 2010). My friend Shaun King recruited people worldwide via Twitter to help provide relief to Haiti in January 2010. He later developed a website, www.ahomeinhaiti.org, to provide tents for people who had no place to call home. Within hours of the Nashville flood in May 2010, volunteers were mobilized and donations poured in at an unprecedented speed in large part due to social networks (Axton 2010). This was a "boom" heard around the world.

It's clear that we can leverage social media to advance the kingdom of God in this generation. The question is, will you join in?

#Facebook

"Quit counting fans, followers and blog subscribers like bottle caps. Think, instead, about what you're hoping to achieve with and through the community that actually cares about what you're doing."

—Amber Naslund of Social Media Today

Chances are you've heard about Facebook. Facebook is the world's most popular social networking website. It allows users to create profiles, add friends, send messages, and share photos. Users can join networks within Facebook by city, workplace, school, and region. In this chapter I'll help get you started in setting up your own Facebook profile and help you create a Facebook page for your ministry or organization.

CREATING A FACEBOOK PAGE

1. Register your account. Go to Facebook.com. Fill out the form on that page. You need to include your email address so that Facebook can confirm your registration and send you future updates from your profile. Next, enter a password of your choice, your sex, and your birthday. Then hit the "Sign Up" button at the bottom of the page.

2. Confirm your email. Facebook will now tell you it has sent a confirmation email to your email account. Go find this email, click on the link it provides, and it will take you to your new Facebook profile.

3. Find your friends and family. You'll have to go through a series of steps to personalize your profile.

First, Facebook will offer to scour your email address book for others already using the site whom you can invite to be your friends. Simply enter your email address and password, and Facebook will find your friends. Select the ones you want to add by ticking the boxes to the left of their pictures, and then click "Add to Friends" at the bottom.

WHY DOES FACEBOOK WANT MY BIRTHDATE?

Later we're going to talk about privacy issues on Facebook, but for now let me assure you that you can protect your birthdate if you do not want others to view it. There are several reasons Facebook requires this information. First, there are certain age requirements for particular networks within Facebook, and the website must be able to verify the right users are accessing these networks. Second, Facebook is free to use, which means advertisers pay for the site through their ad dollars. They use your demographic information to determine which ads to show you. Over the years it has been possible to sign up for Facebook without leaving some of this info, and other times it has not been possible. If you're uncomfortable giving this information, there's nothing to stop you from trying to sign up without it, but it might not work.

You can also choose friends from your email address book who aren't on Facebook. The system will send them an email inviting them to join up and be your friend.

4. Find classmates and co-workers. Click on "Find Friends" in the top right-hand corner and fill in the various fields such as "Hometown," "Current City," "High School," "College or University," "Employer," and "Graduate School." Now select anyone you recognize or want as a friend and click "Add to Friends." Sometimes when you add a friend, you'll have to write the text from the security box into the text box to confirm.

5. Join a regional network. You cannot view other people's profiles if you are not friends with them unless you are both in the same regional network. Joining a regional network means it's easier to track down friends. On your Facebook setup homepage, there is the option to enter a city or town. Enter in your home city and click "Join."

6. Edit your profile. Click your name in the upper right-hand corner. You'll see that all the sections on this page are empty. Click "Edit Profile" and you can enter personal details about yourself. Once you are happy with your entries, click "save changes." Remember, you can always go back and edit your details whenever you want.

The next section on the left-hand column is "Profile Picture." Here you can upload a picture that will appear when others view your profile. This picture will also be in the upper left-hand corner when you are viewing your own home page—also called a "News Feed"—where you see posts from all of your friends.

Another way for people to learn about you is through your relatives. The next section, called "Friends and Family," allows you to add family members along with their relation to you on your profile page.

In the next few sections, "Education and Work," "Philosophy," "Arts and Entertainment," "Sports," and "Activities and Interests," you can enter miscellaneous information such as hobbies, religious and political views, favorite movies and music, etc. Most people enter details as a list, but keep in mind, the longer it is, the less likely people are to read it. If you want to make your Facebook profile reflect your personality and you want people to read it, then keep it short and interesting. Irony is widely used in this section, so don't be afraid to be silly and have a laugh as you would with friends. While filling out sections like "education" and "work" will help other people find you, remember that you don't have to fill out every field.

Finally, click on "Contact Information." If you like, you can enter email addresses, your phone number, instant messaging screen names, your mailing address, and even links to your websites, such as blogs. Remember, even though your friends are the only ones who can view your profile info, Facebook is public, so think about it before you enter certain personal information. Be sure to save your changes when you are done.

FACEBOOK PAGES VS. FACEBOOK GROUPS

Aside from your profile, there are other ways you can create a presence on Facebook: by creating pages and groups. Facebook pages are really just an adaptation of your profile page. Most pastors or church leaders that I know who have a Facebook page (often referred to as a "fan page") do so because their Facebook profile has too many friends (a Facebook profile can only hold five thousand friends, while pages allow you an unlimited number of fans).

Groups are very different though. They function as a community within a community. You can currently have a group that is "secret," which basically means that postings from your group will not display in the News Feed of all your friends' Facebook profiles. My ministry currently has a generic page for the ministry itself, and then I created a Facebook group specifically for the small-group Bible study that I am in. The "secret group" allows us to be able to post prayer requests and other things that members might not want made public. One thing to keep in mind is that posts made in your group do NOT post as updates in the News Feed, which means others can't join your group unless you invite them.

CREATING A FACEBOOK PAGE FOR YOUR MINISTRY

1. Find the Facebook link to create a page. There are several ways to set up a Facebook page. Go to http://www.facebook.com/pages/create.php or scroll to the very bottom of your profile and click "Create a

Page" in the bottom left-hand corner. You can also go to http://www.facebook.com. Underneath the sign-up area, click on the link that says "Create a page for a celebrity, band or business."

2. Name your Facebook page and select a category. This step requires some careful thought, as this is the only information that *cannot* be changed at a later stage. The only way to change anything you select here is to delete your page and start from scratch—a minor annoyance if you make a mistake in the initial set-up before you have fans, but a big deal if you decide you want something different a few months down the line when your page is well established.

For a small business, begin by clicking "Local business or place" and choose the most appropriate category from the drop-down menu. Once you've done this, you'll be asked to enter the name of your page. Here, many people make the mistake of entering a description of their business rather than the actual business name. While a description does tell people what you do, this dilutes your branding. You can also add your company's address and phone number.

3. Adding more information. When you're done entering your business's basic information, you'll then be prompted to add a photo for your business. If you have a business logo, use this as the picture on your page. You may also choose to use a picture of yourself here if you are strongly identified with the business brand. Next it will ask you to describe your business and add a website. The last step before creating your page is to claim any smaller or illegitimate pages with the same name. You can skip this step or choose pages to claim from the

Facebook-generated list. After hitting either "Save Info" or "Skip," you will be directed to your new page!

4. The "About" box. This box is found underneath the picture and provides a quick snapshot of your business or ministry. You can use this box for your tagline or to provide a quick summary of your ministry or to highlight important keywords related to the products or services you offer.

5. Become a "fan" of your own page. The first fan of your business is a very important person: you! Click on the link at the top of the page to add yourself as a fan. This action will appear in your personal profile News Feed and be visible to your friends—an excellent way to alert people to the existence of your page.

6. Invite friends to become fans of your page. Underneath the "Messages" section on the right is an area called "Invite Friends." Here Facebook has suggested friends for you to invite to join your page. You can invite anyone you are friends with by clicking the "See All" button, also in the "Invite Friends" section.

And there you have it, the basics of creating a Facebook page for your ministry!

CREATING A FACEBOOK GROUP FOR YOUR MINISTRY

Creating a Facebook group is very easy if you already have an account. If you don't have an account, revisit how to set up a Facebook profile page earlier in this chapter.

1. You must have a Facebook account. It is a good idea to build up your profile page there first before creating a group. People will always look at the profile of someone before deciding to join a group.

2. Create group. Next, look for the "Create Group" button; this is on the left-hand side of your News Feed under "Groups." Once you have clicked, the next page will ask you to create a group name, add members, and choose privacy settings. There are three levels of privacy:

- **Open**—This is probably the one you want. When you have the group up and ready to accept new members, they can join instantly and can see all the parts of your group.

- **Closed**—Members cannot join this group until they have requested it, and until an admin (you) has allowed them access.

- **Secret**—This can be a useful option if you need to gather some good content before you open your group. No one can see it while it is secret.

3. Icon. Choose one of the dozens of icons to set your group apart from others on Facebook.

4. Adding information and changing settings. By clicking the gear in the upper right-hand corner, you can add a description to your group. From here you can also change the name of your group, adjust your group's privacy settings, create a group email, and change posting and membership settings. It's probably a good idea to turn them all on—this will allow members to add photos, videos, and links. Enabling members to interact within your group is key. You want to add a lot of interactivity to your group. You can also make members into officers here, which mainly means adding labels to the best contributors in your group. Now let's go over what you can add to your Facebook group. Note that Facebook is always updating these features, and by the time you read this they will likely have new items not mentioned here.

Videos: Videos related to your subject can make your group an important focal point; it can become a place to go for more information. The most useful and engaging videos work the best: create humorous, instructional, newsy, insightful, or any other type of video you can think of. Try lots of variations.

Photos: Photos related to your site's content work quite well too and these could be tied into your videos and provide insights into you or some area that your group relates to.

AN IMPORTANT NOTE: If you choose to set up a group, you have to keep updating it. If you don't, people will get bored and not come back. The trick is to just be yourself; be polite, friendly, and reply to anyone who leaves a link, photo, or wall comment so they know there's a real person on the other end of the conversation.

Below your group members' pictures you have a few options to edit your group and use some other features. Here are a few:

Chat: This is exactly what it says. You can keep group members updated with what's going on with your group with a simple message. If you have events going on, a newsletter coming out, or something else of great importance for your group to announce, this is where you set that up.

Suggest members: You can use this area to invite others to join your group. Maybe you have Facebook friends on your personal profile who may be interested in your group. This is your chance to invite them.

Event: This is where you can create a related event that may be of interest to your friends who may not necessarily be in your group. Maybe you've organized a get-together in person at a selected venue; perhaps you're organizing an online video chat or something else that relates to your group. This is how to announce it with specific dates and times.

Leave group: This only applies to others (you are the administrator after all), so don't click it!

That pretty much covers setting up a group in Facebook. Here's to great community!

5

#Twitter

"Stop Marketing.
Start Engaging!"

—Scott Stratten

Twitter is considered microblogging at its finest. Do you have an appreciation for people who are concise or brief? If you nod your head "yes," then you'll love Twitter. On Twitter you have to say what you need to say in just one hundred forty characters or less. It's all about less clutter.

I currently have around fifteen thousand people who follow me (@terracecrawford) on Twitter. In other words, about fifteen thousand people have acknowledged that they want to listen in and engage with me in conversation. I can't begin to tell you how many personal connections I have made through this one social media platform alone. And to be honest, it's probably my favorite social media platform. I have seen people moved to action. I have seen people help meet financial needs, seen prayer answered, and more!

Twitter's tagline used to be "What's happening?" Each day millions of users answer this question through short posts (called "tweets") in just one hundred forty characters or less!

Here are some sample tweets:

"Just sippin' my latte at Starbucks."

"Just got home from the dentist. No cavities! #success"

"Did anyone catch the Cowboys vs. Skins game last night? Absolutely incredible."

"That's fabulous, Terrace," you are probably saying to yourself right now (humor me, OK?). "How do I get on Twitter?"

I'm glad you asked.

HOW TO CREATE A TWITTER ACCOUNT

1. Signing up on Twitter. Go to www.twitter.com. The signup page is right on the front page. You can't miss it.

2. Choosing your Twitter username. In the first field you will need to fill out your full name. It is best to use your real name here because people will want to locate you. Your username—what you'll create in the next step—can be a nickname or something unique, although I'd encourage you to use your real name here too (i.e.:@terracecrawford). If you are creating an account for your church or ministry, I would encourage your username to be the official name of your church or ministry. You can change your username in the account settings at any time.

3. Provide an email address. You'll want to set up a way for Twitter to notify you when you have a message (be patient—we're getting to that). So enter the email address you use the most. Once you set up your account, you will need to confirm your email address before your Twitter account is active.

4. Selecting your interests. Twitter will use your selections to generate a list of suggested accounts you might like to "follow." Once you're getting started you will see other people who are on Twitter with a "follow" icon next to their username. If you click the follow button, you will essentially subscribe to their feed, and their posts will begin showing up in your home page feed.

5. Find friends on Twitter. One of the things Twitter will ask you is to "find friends." You can type in your email information and Twitter will scan your email account to find out who you already know on Twitter. You have the option to select the blue "Follow All" button on the right-hand side of the results, or if you would like to be more selective you could choose to follow people individually by using the gray "send request" button.

6. Personalizing your account. Two key agenda items here: (1) You need to upload a nice picture of yourself. (2) You need to write a mini bio for yourself (something that states who you are or what you do). You are only allowed one hundred sixty words here, so keep your text simple and direct. You can make a big difference by adding a few more personal words. Don't let this worry you, though, you can always come back to it. Some people keep this area to a minimum anyway and state something they like or dislike in life (i.e.: "I like bacon"). You can't argue with that one, can you?

You should definitely indicate a website URL for your ministry or blog address so that people can connect with you beyond Twitter. Twitter will also provide a place to indicate your geographical location; you should indicate this to connect with people in your area.

7. Create a background. Your profile is almost ready, but it would be nice if you didn't leave it naked. Why not dress it up a bit? Create a custom background for your Twitter page. To begin customizing your background, hover over the person icon in the top right-hand corner, click on "Settings" and then "Design." Twitter will offer you a number of backgrounds to choose from. If you want, you can upload your own photos or graphics in the Twitter format. If your account is not for personal use, but rather for your ministry or organization's use, you might choose a picture or create a custom background that reflects your ministry. Additionally, you can configure the color of the text, links, sidebars, etc.

8. Learn by example. Before you start tweeting, it's a good idea to get familiar with what everyone is talking about. Visit the Twitter accounts of people you know by name (celebrity, family member, or friend). Just type their name in the "Search" field and get a look at what they are tweeting about. Once you read a few of their tweets, you'll see just how this works. Then go ahead and post your first tweet. Remember, this is microblogging at its finest, so you're limited to one hundred forty characters.

HOW TO TWEET

You have several options for how to send a tweet. If you're on the go a lot, you'll most likely want to send and receive updates from your mobile phone. If you're at a desk for most of the day, you might want to use your computer or a third-party application. Since most new Twitter users rely on their desktop computers, we'll start there.

- **Browser-based tweets.** Open your Internet browser and log on to your Twitter account (www.Twitter.com/youraccountname). Use the "Compose new Tweet" box in the right-hand corner to enter a message. Click the "Tweet" button and your tweet is sent out to the Internet. Your tweet will show up in your followers' home page feed. You can send as many tweets as you want, as often as you like, but remember—most people will not want to hear from you every few minutes, so slow your roll!

- **Replying to tweets.** You will sometimes see a tweet you want to reply to in your home page feed. This is easy to do. When you type the "@" symbol along with the user's name (@terracecrawford), your reply will show up on their Twitter page as well as on yours. Unless a person has a protected account, everything you send with an @ reply (spoken as an "at reply") will be seen by everyone on Twitter.

- **The direct message.** Sometimes you might prefer to send a private message rather than a public message. In Twitter lingo this is called a "direct message." This is a private tweet that will not be visible by anyone who views your Twitter home page or the home page of the person you sent the direct message to. To send a direct message to someone, they must first be following you on Twitter. If you try to send a direct message to someone you don't follow, Twitter will politely remind you that you can't do that. The nice thing about this (and maybe the *only* nice thing) is that this prevents people from spamming you.

To send a direct message you can simply type "D" (space) and then the @username of the person you want to send a message to. Unfortunately, you are still limited to one hundred forty characters of content, but you can send multiple DMs to someone. When I do this I typically type "cont." at the end of each tweet so it informs the recipient that these tweets are continued.

- **Shortening your tweet links.** I do like the brevity of Twitter, but the one hundred forty character limit forces you to choose your words wisely. Sometimes it prevents you from including a link to a website or two. For instance, if you had a news story you wanted to tweet but the URL was ridiculously long, you would not have much room for your personal commentary given the character limitation. In cases like this you can use helpful web applications such as TinyURL.com or Bit.ly. On these sites you simply copy and paste the long URL into the window indicated, and after clicking "shorten," your link will shorten. You can also choose the new URL so that it's easier to read or understand. Then just copy and paste this link into your tweet, and readers will be able to click it to go to the location where you are directing them.

- **Mobile tweeting.** When you set up your mobile phone in your Twitter settings, you will be able to send tweets directly from that device. After you have configured your settings, you will be able to text your tweet to 40404. Twitter will then recognize your phone number and update your Twitter account for the world to see your message. If you have a smartphone, you should download an app specifically for this purpose. This will allow you to push your tweets directly through the application rather than having to text them.

There are dozens of Twitter apps out there. Just enter "Twitter apps" as a web search and you'll get thousands of hits, with the most popular rated accordingly. Read and choose the one you like.

POPULAR THINGS YOU'LL SEE ON TWITTER

1. The hashtag. Hashtags are basically words with no spaces following a "#" sign. They were created to help group topics in Twitter. For instance, quite often at a conference you'll see attenders tweeting "#nameofconference." If you type #nameofconference in the search bar on Twitter or at search.Twitter.com, you will get a running thread (in real time) of what people are saying about the conference. Of course, they have to remember to include the hashtag word in their tweet or the search won't add their tweet to the list.

There are other cases where people create hashtags (sometimes really long ones) for no reason other than to editorialize or to be funny. For example, one day I randomly tweeted #icouldeatbaconalldaylong. Even though I don't owe an explanation for my love for bacon, I included this at the end of a tweet update.

2. The RT (retweet). A retweet is when you read something another Twitter user has shared and you decide that you want to share that with your followers. You can use the "Retweet" button or link to retweet that information to your followers. Two ways that I usually structure my tweets are as follows:

RT @terracecrawford: The more mature I grow, the more sensitive I'll be to sin in my own life, and less focused on the faults of others.—Rick Warren

Or like this:

The more mature I grow, the more sensitive I'll be to sin in my own life, and less focused on the faults of others.—Rick Warren (via @terracecrawford)

3. #FF or #FollowFriday. I'm not really sure who started this but I like it. #FF stands for Follow Friday. On Fridays you may see other Twitter users suggesting people they think you should follow. Their tweet will list the Twitter names of people they are recommending along with the hashtag #FF or #FollowFriday.

4. Tweetup. "Tweetups" are face-to-face meetings or gatherings held by Twitter users. I suppose anyone could organize it, but you might want to do a search on Twitter for your city to see if someone has already coordinated an effort like this.

5. Favorite. Twitter allows you to bookmark, save, or "favorite" tweets. You can store your tweets in a list and people can even browse your favorites. You can favorite a tweet by clicking on the little star that appears when you hover over a tweet in your Twitter feed.

SETTING UP A TWITTER LIST

Twitter users can organize others into groups, or lists, that can help you filter the tweets you are receiving. It also helps make your time on Twitter more efficient.

1. Create a list. To create a new Twitter list, simply follow these instructions:

- Navigate to your lists page (for direct access, go to Twitter.com/lists). This can be done via the profile drop-down menu in the top navigation bar or by going to your profile page and clicking the "Lists" tab.

- Click "Create list." Enter the name of your list (note: list names cannot exceed twenty-five characters, nor can they begin with a numerical character), a short description of the list you are creating, and whether you want the list to be private (only viewable by you) or public, meaning that anyone can subscribe to or follow the list.

- Click "Save list."

2. Adding or removing people from your lists. You can add users to your lists from anywhere you see the person icon drop-down (looks like a silhouette). This includes the following: people searches, profile pages, followers, and following lists. To add or remove users from your lists, follow these simple steps:

- Click the person icon; this brings up a drop-down menu.

- Select "Add" or "Remove from lists."

- A pop-up will appear displaying your created lists. Check the lists to which you would like to add the user, or uncheck the lists from which you'd like to remove the user.

- To check to see if the user you wanted to add was successfully included in that list, navigate to the "lists" tab on your profile page. Click the desired list, then click "members." The person will appear in the list of members.

3. Viewing your lists. To view the stream of tweets from any group of people in the lists you follow or have created, follow these steps:

- Go to your profile page.

- Click the "Lists" tab on the left panel of the screen.

- Choose which list you'd like to view.

- Right away, you'll see a stream of tweets from the users included in that list.

4. Editing or deleting lists. To edit or delete a list, follow these steps:

- Go to your profile page.

- Click the "Lists" tab on the left panel of the screen. You will see lists you've created and other people's lists you follow.

- Select which list you'd like to edit or delete from the lists you've created.

- Click "Edit" to update your list credentials or click "Delete" to remove the list entirely.

Note: You cannot add or remove people from your list on this page—you must do that from the profile pages of each individual you wish to add or delete. See above.

5. Subscribing to/following other people's lists. Following a list is as simple as following any other Twitter user.

- Click on the "Lists" tab when viewing their profiles, and select which list you'd like to subscribe to.

- From the list page, click "Subscribe" to follow the list. You can also consequently remove yourself from a list by blocking the creator of the list.

HOW TO SEND TWEETS TO FACEBOOK

Twitter has made it easier to send tweets to your Facebook profile. All you have to do is click one single button. Here's how:

1. Log in to your Twitter account.

2. Click "Settings" and then click "Profile." This will then allow you the opportunity to edit your profile.

3. Scroll down to the bottom of this page and click the button that says "Post your tweets to Facebook."

Note: you must also be signed into Facebook for this to work. If you're not, you'll be asked to sign in and give your permission to the app before it will work.

As a word of warning: Twitter and Facebook are two different networks with two different types of syntax and etiquette. It isn't always advisable to connect one network to another for fear of alienating your connections on both.

A TWITTER STRATEGY FOR CHURCHES

If your church or ministry decides to use Twitter, it would first be wise to decide how you want to leverage it, or what your strategy is, as you get started. Ask questions like: How will our Twitter account be used? What will we communicate to our followers? Who decides what kinds of messages we communicate?

Being able to clearly communicate your strategy to your leadership (unless you are the leadership) is of utmost importance, just like it is for every social media platform outlined in this book. Once you know the benefits of using Twitter (and you're not just creating an account to create an account), you'll be able to roll out a plan to your staff and let them know what is expected. You may discover that Twitter can save you time in communicating with your congregation over other communication channels, like email. Here are a few quick things that might be of interest to you as your ministry considers using Twitter:

1. Quick ministry updates. Twitter can be used for quick (and important) updates to your church congregation. For instance, if your church needed to cancel weekend services due to snow, you could send out a simple update to let everyone know about the cancellation.

You could also set up multiple accounts for different ministries in your church. For security purposes, I'd recommend only a couple of people having the authorization to update your accounts.

2. Reinforcing the message. Twitter is an excellent platform for helping reinforce your teaching from the weekend. A pastor can use his or her personal account (or church Twitter account) to send thoughtful questions or insights throughout the week. Another interesting way that some church leaders are using Twitter is by sending daily scriptures.

3. Users can "Follow" via text message. One of the neat things about Twitter is the "fast follow" feature. If your church decides to use this platform, you might have trouble getting everyone on Twitter. No worries! You can tell anyone that they can receive the tweets on their phone (sent via text/SMS message). All they have to do is subscribe to your user account by sending a text message (from their mobile phones). Instruct people to text "Follow @username" to Twitter at 40404 and they will instantly start receiving SMS alerts for that user's tweets.

WHY CHURCH LEADERS FAIL WITH SOCIAL MEDIA

1. They become narcissistic. It's easy for your head to swell once you start attracting followers on social media platforms. Some leaders have the tendency to talk about themselves too much. Be careful of becoming narcissistic. Stay grounded and engage with your followers.

2. They embarrass themselves. Many leaders have gotten themselves into trouble by forgetting that what they post to Facebook and Twitter can be seen by everyone. Remember that social media is known for the "quick" updates, so think carefully before you post. Never post when you're angry or frustrated. Don't criticize others. Don't post something that might embarrass you, your family, or anyone else.

3. Become unresponsive. Failing to return calls or emails is just bad protocol. The same principle is also true for your social networks. If you only check your social media accounts once every two weeks, it's going to hurt your relationships, and your readers or subscribers may drop off. If you don't reply to private/direct messages, don't comment when people post to your Facebook wall, and don't respond (even with something short) when people reply to your Twitter updates, people are going to interact with you less or may even assume you're straight up ignoring them and take offense.

4. They are not living authentic lives. Church leaders sometimes think they have to be perfect. The truth is, nobody is perfect, and everyone knows it. If you act like everything is good all the time, people will perceive you as inauthentic. If you act as if you never make mistakes and know all the answers, you make it harder for others to talk about their mistakes, and you make it harder for others to be honest when they're experiencing doubts and uncertainty. Don't be afraid to show some transparency online. Have candid conversations and help people.

5. Debate and divide. Online (and offline) debates rarely cause anyone to shift their position on an issue. Discussion is great, but if things get heated or personal, it's time to lighten up. Political issues can be particularly divisive. It's one thing to talk about the way your faith impacts your view of issues, but when discussion drifts toward specific leaders, candidates, and parties, you run the risk of alienating half your congregation. Be careful of engaging in debates, particularly online when perception is everything.

6. Become a part of the morality police. Your virtual friends and followers are not perfect. You may even have a pretty healthy following of people who don't have a relationship with Jesus Christ. Many of them are going to swear, post questionable pictures of themselves, and share things you don't agree with. If something is really offensive, consider contacting the person privately about it, but don't call out people publicly.

#Blogs

"Blogging is simply a new way of telling stories. In the same way that we seek out new modes of worshipping, preaching and reaching out, we must find new methods of sharing stories. The message doesn't change when the methodology changes. If the methodology fails to change, however, we begin to distance ourselves from the people we are called to reach, and we risk becoming irrelevant."

—Bailey and Storch

HOW BLOGS WORK

A blog might be best described as an online journal entry for the world to view. "Blog posts" are typically published with the most recent entry first. There are a number of features that set blogs apart from other websites. Here are a few:

Style: Blogs tend to be written from a personal perspective and are usually written in a more conversational style. They can be written by one person or sometimes even a team of people.

Topic: Blog topics can vary from a churchy topic to something very comical that has nothing to do with your faith.

Links and trackbacks: Blogging platforms usually offer services that not only allow people to write blogs but also make it very easy for them to insert links to other websites, usually in reference to an article or blog post or to provide further information about the specific subject matter.

Comments: Each blog post has a comments section that will allow readers of your post to leave messages about your articles. The comments will vary in number depending on the size of your audience or how much traffic your specific post gets. Some church leaders prefer to turn off the comments feature on their blogs, but be aware that doing so shuts down the community and conversation.

Subscription: Another thing that sets blogs apart from websites is that a blog can be subscribed to, usually via Real Simple Syndication

(RSS) technology. This makes it easy for the reader to keep up with the content.

Distribution: Uploading the content on your blog is only part of what you need to do. You also need to think about how your message is distributed. It's likely that few people will actually visit your site each day as compared with those who will subscribe in a newsreader application (see "reading blogs" in the next section). RSS notifies a newsreader or your personal homepage that there is new content available and forwards the text and images.

Reading blogs: You can read blogs directly on the website where they are posted, but it's far easier to use a newsreader application. It is important for RSS feeds to work with your newsreader because these programs make it much easier for blogs and other social media users to become part of communities. They may be small communities, but to their users they may be highly relevant and valuable. The most popular reader is the Google Reader, although there are many other readers available. I'll discuss how to set up your newsreader in just a bit.

You can find blogs on topics you're interested in by using search engines like Technorati.com or Google Blog Search. When you're on a blog that is particularly interesting or relevant to you, look for something like "blogroll." It's a list of recommended blogs and is a great way of exploring the networks of blogs.

HOW TO CREATE A BLOG

1. Decide what you'll write about and who you are writing to. Don't overthink this one. You don't have to have all the details figured out to start a blog. Although marketers will tell you to pick a very niche topic, I know tons of great, popular bloggers who just write about their lives and experiences or post pictures and videos of things they like. If in doubt, pick a general direction and get started. Your blog will naturally evolve over time. Once you start writing, you'll start to realize what you truly enjoy writing about versus what you thought you'd enjoy writing about. Ideas will come to you at strange times, and you'll have more to say than you thought. Note: if your end goal is to monetize your blog, consider writing about products you can sell as an affiliate, topics that you could teach classes about or create e-books and information products about. Or, consider writing for demographics that are highly valued by advertisers.

2. Buy a domain name. Anyone can buy a domain name, and everyone who is even thinking about starting a blog, business, or building a personal brand should buy a domain name. For instance, I use terracecrawford.com as the domain name for my blog, but there are numerous providers you can buy one from. Simply do a web search on "register domain names" and you'll see pages and pages of places where you can buy yours. The prices may vary, so it's worth comparison-shopping. If you have a particular domain name that you'd like to secure, I'd encourage you to go purchase it right now. Doing so will reserve it for your use for a specific length of time.

Here's an assortment of possible blog types for your ministry:

A sermon or teaching series blog. Some churches create blogs for specific teaching or sermon series and offer a podcast or text version of the sermon. If you are not the senior leader in your church, you could always present this as an idea at your next church staff meeting.

A children's ministry blog. Create a space for your children's ministry where leaders and parents can provide insight, care, and announcements for your church's children's ministry. Mommy blogs typically have pretty solid audiences, so a blog centered around the kids in your church has incredible potential. Chances are you might already have a mommy-blogger in your church who could help you with the blog!

A student ministry blog. Some youth and student ministries are foregoing websites for their ministries and are using blogs instead. You might even choose to have a student ministry website and create a blog for parents only.

Community blog. This type of blog may replace your old-school church newsletter. Your church attenders may just love a blog where they can read announcements about church events. Commenting may be turned off for this one and authorship privileges given to all church leaders to post upcoming announcements or events. This blog could have a forum-like or a wiki feel to it. Just makes sure to keep it up to date.

Information technology blog. Create a space for the geeks and techies at your church to exchange information about keeping all systems up and running. I personally love reading blogs like this because they are informative and teach me a lot about media in the church. Bloggers could offer lots of behind-the-scenes posts that could not only serve those who work with technology at your church but also help church leaders around the world who serve in this capacity.

Staff blogs. A place where staffers can speak with an authentic voice and nurture the dialogue so many of us hunger for. Many ministers aren't ready to do this, but it's neat when more than one person on a church staff blogs. Ask your fellow staff pastors if they have an interest in blogging and share with them what you already know.

Buying a domain name will also allow you to have a custom email address (yourname@yourdomain.com instead of yourname@gmail.com). It looks more professional and it is pretty easy to set up. Once you buy your domain name, go to "manage domains" and you should see an option called "Email Forwarding Setup." Enter the email address you want and where it should be forwarded (to your primary email address).

What if you can't get the name you want? You can always consider buying a domain name with a different extension other than .com. For example, .org, .tv, .biz, .me, and .info are also popular choices.

3. Set up hosting. Every blog needs a host. Here's an analogy that may help you understand a little better. Just like you need land before you can build a house, you can't build a website unless you have a place to put it. So think of your website host as the land, your domain name as the house, and the content of your website (articles, pictures, graphics) as your furniture and belongings.

Self-hosted vs. WordPress-hosted blogs. If you get your blog at Word-Press.com, your blog is hosted by WordPress. This means the hosting is free—WordPress will provide updates, upgrades, backups, and site security. In other words, choosing WordPress.com is the way to get your site running within minutes without any technical knowledge. Other simple, hosted blog sites include Typepad, Blogger, and Tumblr.

Those who choose a site other than these will still probably want to use the free WordPress software but will need to maintain the updates and other services independently. Hosting usually costs about $60-$80 per year, depending on which provider you use.

A self-hosted blog. If you think you'd like to grow a big following or even use your blog for business purposes someday, it's wise to use a self-hosted blog. It may seem more expensive and intimidating up front, but it gives you several more options right from the start.

With a self-hosted blog you can install plug-ins that greatly enhance your site. You can think of plug-ins kind of like iPhone apps—there are some amazing plug-ins out that really enhance the functionality and customization of your site. If you aren't self-hosted, you can't add plug-ins to your site. With a self-hosted site, you can completely customize your site's design, whereas WordPress.com sites are limited to premade themes only.

Plug-ins. The list of plug-ins is seemingly endless, but some popular types include spam blockers (for comments), search engine optimization, social media and sharing buttons, and ratings for your posts.

4. Selecting a host. If you choose to self-host your website, you're going to need a service for it. Do an Internet search on "web hosting" and you'll find many potential hosts, as well as other sites offering reviews of various hosts. One of the most important parts of your hosting package is customer service. Often when I think I have an issue with my website, I find that it's a simple lack of understanding of how certain technology/processes work. You'll probably call your host often in the beginning, and that's OK. You'll learn a lot by spending some time with customer service.

You may want to buy the basic package from your web host each year so you don't have to worry about renewing it. One year of hosting may cost you between $60-80 per year. Once you've purchased your package, sign into your control panel (c-panel) using the information your host sent you in your welcome email. It will include your login name, password, and the URL to access your host. Just remember to keep this information handy for later use. Scroll to the bottom of the control panel and click "Quick Install" then select "WordPress."

5. Add information and write your first post. Once people start reading your blog, they'll want to know who you are and how they can reach you. Be sure you've created an "about" page, preferably with your picture, and a "contact" page. Include your social media contact info too. If you're not comfortable posting your email address, create a contact form (for free) by using Wufoo.com. Creating forms with that tool is easy and all you have to do is copy and paste the code into the page where you want it. When people submit the contact form, Wufoo will forward you their inquiry via email.

FIVE TIPS TO HELP MAKE YOUR BLOG SIMPLE AND SLICK

1. Pick a theme. What do you think my primary colors are for my blog? Stop reading for a second and go to www.terracecrawford.com. If you notice, I have three primary colors running on my site. This is something that people notice. Your colors and theme should be consistent on your site.

2. Customize it. Branding yourself is important. One way to do this is by customizing your site in simple, yet professional ways. You can start doing this by customizing your header. Also, make it easy for people to know *who* they are reading. Yesterday I visited a blog and it took me seven clicks to find out *who* was the author of the blog. When people visit blogs, they like to know right away who the author is. You might find that your "about me" page is one of the most frequently visited pages on your blog.

3. Go BIG. Fourteen different fonts on your blog is thirteen too many. Try to stick with one primary font. If you want readers to find your blog easier to read, increase the font size a bit. The font size on my blog used to be very small. Then I learned that people really like larger fonts! Go big or go home, as they say, no?

4. Keep it simple. Keep your blog posts short. Don't clutter up your site. Use readable fonts. Run with a stripped-down layout. These are things that make your blog simple, and simple is best. Recently a well-known leader asked me about my blog. He said of the blogs he reads that he likes mine the best. After naming off the other blogs that show up in his read, I was curious to know why mine was his favorite. "Your blog is simple," he said. "I like simple."

5. Make it slick. My favorite blogs are those that mix it up a little. Often you'll read a text post, sometimes you'll view a video, and occasionally you'll see pictures or slick graphics.

SO WHAT SHOULD YOU WRITE (BLOG) ABOUT?

It all depends on your audience. When I started blogging, my blog was newsier than anything. I blogged about my life or world affairs. When I realized I might be the only person reading my blog, I decided to start blogging about things that interested me, like youth ministry and leadership. Soon after I changed topics, I began to notice that other like-minded people wanted to be a part of the conversation too.

If you're not yet familiar with Christian blogs, I suggest you visit http://christian-church.alltop.com. AllTop does a great job of aggregating the top one hundred sites in just about every category. There you will find one hundred Christian church leader blogs. After you begin reading those, start leaving comments. Join the conversation and become a part of the community.

BLOGGING ETIQUETTE

Blogging comes with its own set of rules, guidelines, and governing principles. Many of these you just have to figure out on your own, but there has been a lot written on the topic too. In your journey to be a great blogger, try to remember these etiquette tips:

1. Give some link love. If what another blogger wrote inspires you and if it's appropriate to your blog, make mention of their post in one of your posts. Providing links to articles and sites is a great way to promote your community and group of blogging friends.

2. Original recipe. Do not plagiarize someone else's content or ideas. Putting a new spin on a subject is one thing, but copying someone else's ideas is not right. Be original.

3. Check yourself (and your grammar). Although some typos may slip through, try your hardest to provide a post with proper grammar and spelling. Your blog is a reflection of you and your credibility. If necessary, have someone proofread for you.

4. Respond to commenters. A short thank-you is sufficient if you have nothing more to say. However, comment sections often end up being the meat of the post. Many church leaders will opt out of using comment fields, but allowing comments on your posts is a vital part of community-building.

5. Keep negativity to yourself. Your comment is a reflection of you. Negative comments decrease your chances of receiving visitors from other sites. Just like anywhere else, my particular experience has been that the nastiest comments often come from anonymous commenters. If someone leaves a negative comment on your blog, do not feel obligated to leave it in the comment section. A negative comment can change the dynamics of the other valuable comments. Feel free to delete it or mark it as spam.

6. Inquiries. Chances are you will get emails (and maybe some letters) from readers. Be prepared to handle these and make sure you respond in kind.

7. No spamming. Overusing the name of another blogger in comments and/or posts is often considered content or comment spam. Unscrupulous bloggers do this intentionally to raise the visibility of their blogs in a Google search.

8. No dead links. Consistently providing links that do not lead to their intended location is frustrating to your readers and can lead to a loss of credibility. This sometimes happens when what your link originally pointed to on another blog gets moved. If one of your commenters sends you a note informing you of a dead link, fix it right away.

9. Return the favor. If someone visits your blog and leaves a comment, it's good manners to visit their blog as well. If you cannot identify with their most current post, browse through their archives and find one about which you can leave a short comment.

10. Off the subject. Do not comment on someone's blog without reading the title and the complete post. A poorly written, off-subject comment leaves others confused and can damage your credibility.

SEARCH ENGINE OPTIMIZATION

When you are starting out with social media, it's best to avoid flowery metaphors and to be practical with the title of your blog. Keep it simple, like only using your church name. One reason for this is search engine optimization (SEO).

Search engines, like Google, are always combing the web trying to index sites to make it easier for people to find them. This is great news for you. You want people to be able to find you on a search engine, so it is important to keep SEO in the back of your mind while blogging and creating your social media profiles. This also means that in your blogs you need to provide Google with specific and relevant information. This is easier than you might think, but it requires you to refrain from mentioning your ministries by anything other than their descriptive names. In your blog post, if you refer to your youth ministry as Solid Rock (or whatever your in-house name for it is) the search engines will not tag your post as having anything to do with youth ministry. Someone trying to find out information about your church's youth ministry isn't going to search for your metaphors. Instead they will search keywords like: your church name, youth ministry, the name of your city, your name, etc.

There is a lot to learn about SEO. I have basic information about it on my website or you can Google "SEO" to find more information.

SETTING UP A NEWSREADER

Once you start reading blogs, you'll probably have more than one that you like to read each day, and it is pretty time-consuming to manually visit each site every day. It's most efficient to set up a newsreader that will automatically download all your favorite blog material and organize it for easy reading. Reader applications (also called RSS readers) help you aggregate the feeds of the blogs you like and can be web-based, desktop-based, or even mobile-device-based. To find one that you like, an Internet search on "best newsreader" will provide you with many reviews and "best of" lists. Once you decide what reader you would like to use, you can subscribe to a particular blog's feed by entering the blog's URL into the reader. Once you have done this for all of your favorite blogs, the reader application will aggregate the posts of those blogs whenever they are updated with new information. This is especially helpful in keeping track of bloggers you really like that post infrequently.

Because it's currently free and the most popular reader available, here's how to set up the Google Reader:

- Create a Google account (accounts.Google.com).

- Sign in and go to the reader app (google.com/reader).

- Select "Add Subscription" from the left column.

- Type in the address (or copy and paste from the address bar) of a blog you want to subscribe to and click "Add."

Adding a Subscription from Elsewhere Online

When you are visiting a site to which you want to subscribe, you'll likely see the symbol for RSS, which looks like this: It's often at the right end of the address bar itself. Most sites will also provide a link somewhere else on the page. Sometimes this logo will be highly customized for that particular site, so you might have to look around a bit.

When you click the RSS link, you'll end up on a page that says "Subscribe now" with a number of options to click depending on which reader you use.

Choose the option with the Google logo on it and the next page will allow you to add it to your Google homepage or to your Google Reader account.

Reading Options

You now have a few of your favorite blogs listed in the left column of your Google Reader page. The best way to go through your feeds is up to you. Here are some options:

- "Home," at the top of the left column, lets you review new, unread posts with just a few lines of content from each blog.

- "All Items," just below "Home," is where you can see new, unread posts listed with their complete content.

- Selecting an individual feed from the list in the left column allows you to see new posts as well as scroll down through older ones.

Scanning Options

In the upper right corner you will see tabs for "Expanded view" and "List view." These allow you to toggle between seeing all content as you scroll through your feeds or just titles and the first few words.

Marking as Read

You will mark a post as read when you click on it. Scrolling through posts will also mark them as read, although you have the option to turn this feature off in your settings. Finally, if you want to mark all your new posts as read at once, you can do so at the top of the "All Items" page.

Unsubscribing

If you change your mind about being subscribed to a blog, you can unsubscribe by going to the settings in the upper right corner.

10 TIPS FOR CHURCH BLOGGERS

Many churches have begun creating blogs and incorporating them into their official church websites. I love congregational blogging, but if your ministry isn't there, you might consider a personal blog as a church leader. Either way, here are some tips for church blogging:

1. Clarify your goals. What are you trying to accomplish? It's critical that you understand what are your goals are for your blog. Is your blog to connect with people who go to your church or for outsiders who have never set foot in the door? Different types of ministry blogs have different needs. Ask yourself, "What do we plan to accomplish with this blog?" Once you can answer this, you can answer any number of other questions, such as what your writing style should be, whether it should be invitation-only, whether commenting should be turned on or off, and who is in charge of the content.

2. Become a blog evangelist . . . or find one! Enthusiasm is contagious, and if you are going to create your own blog, it's going to rub off on other people. One way I do this is through commenting on other blogs I like. Do people in your congregation have personal blogs? Subscribe to them and comment on them. You'll be amazed at the communities you'll find, which in turn will give you ideas to build your congregation's blogs.

Additionally, there are many churches that list their staff's personal blogs on their church or ministry websites. This is a great way to connect the people in your church with your staff.

3. Read books on blogging. Remember the story I told about being asked what a blog was? I've learned a lot since then, and much of it has come from reading about the subject. There are a number of books on blogging, one of the best of which is *The Blogging Church* by Brian Bailey. And, of course, the Internet abounds with information on the subject.

4. Focus on your readers. A congregational blog isn't really a personal blog. A congregational blog tends to be a platform where the pastor or staffer writes about church or ministry-related things. Talk to people in the congregation. Look at site statistics. Find out what your congregation would like to have on the website. Some of it may be a match for a blog or two or three. Once you've started a blog, pay attention some more. Find out what's working and what's not, and adjust accordingly.

5. Find a voice for your blog. If you have the time and ability to contribute content to the blog, that's great. But if, like many church leaders, it's all you can do to keep up with daily demands, the key is to find a person who will take charge of the blog once it's in place. Some senior leaders recruit someone to be the voice of their ministry blog. Quite often this person is someone who likes reading blogs or is a tech- or web-savvy person in your church or on your staff.

6. Stakeholder support. Once you have some good ideas, get buy-in from your leadership. Have a meeting to flesh out your plans. Devote some prayer time to direction for your social media ministry and be attentive to what your leadership advises.

7. Remember . . . baby steps! There's rarely a need to hurry the start of a blog. Take time to plan, listen to potential users, and experiment with various technologies. It's an investment that will pay off.

8. Don't deny the power of RSS. RSS feeds are built into all major blog applications. RSS is a phenomenally simple XML standard, and in its simplicity and standardization lie its power. It can be repurposed in all kinds of ways and will save you time and money when keeping up with your blog reading.

9. Host a blogging seminar. You'll have fun and so will those who come. It's a great way to continue building momentum and focusing on your users. If your church doesn't have wireless Internet service, find someplace like a coffee shop that does and get those who can to bring their laptops.

10. Take the plunge . . . start your blog! Earlier I mentioned different options you have for hosted blogs such as Blogger, Tumblr, TypePad, and WordPress. Blogger is astonishingly easy, and even if you don't end up using it yourself, it's good to learn its strengths and weaknesses firsthand so you know when it's the best tool for the job. It's a great starter platform to use. Tumblr is also a nice little platform that is pretty slick and has great character. Many people would say the top blogging platforms are WordPress and TypePad. As you are investigating these, you may come across other services like Joomla or Drupal. When you are beginning, you'll want to simply bypass these options as they are fairly complex and intended for people who know how to code their own websites.

ADDING YOUR BLOG TO YOUR FACEBOOK PAGE

Most of your readers already use Facebook, so it makes sense for them to be able to find you there. One way to do this and also get your blog more exposure is to add it to NetworkedBlogs.com. NetworkedBlogs is a user-generated blog directory and makes it easy to syndicate your feed directly to Twitter and Facebook. Here are a few reasons to add your blog to NetworkedBlogs:

- It's a great way to promote your blog.

- You'll get a your blog listed in their blog directory.

- It easily syndicates your content to your Facebook fan page and personal profile.

- It gives fans an easy way to follow your blog on Facebook where they already are.

- It can add a box of "faces" to your website to display those who are following you.

- It's free for the basic features!

SIGN UP WITH NETWORKEDBLOGS

1. Adding your blog. Start at NetworkedBlogs.com and click the "Add Your Blog" button. You may need to log in to Facebook next.

2. Register your blog. Click the "Register a Blog" button.

3. Blog details. Enter your blog details and follow the prompts. Don't worry, you'll be able to change these details later.

4. Confirmation of authorship. Confirm whether or not you're the blog author. If not, you'll be able to tag the author (if you're friends with the person) or skip that if not.

5. Success! Now you'll see the confirmation page showing your blog is successfully registered with the NetworkedBlogs system.

6. Rate your blog. You may want to rate your blog and invite people to follow, edit, or share now.

SYNDICATING YOUR BLOG ON FACEBOOK

1. In NetworkedBlogs, click the "Syndication" link.

2. Choose your blog. Choose your blog in the drop-down (if you have more than one setup with NetworkedBlogs) then click on the "Add Facebook Target" link.

3. Choose the profile. Now choose the profile where you want your blog posts to show up and click the "add" link for it. It will change to "added" when it's successful.

Now your posts will automatically show up on your profile. You can also set it up to publish to any fan page or group that you're an admin of by following step 3 again.

7

#YouTube

"We're still in the process of picking ourselves up off the floor after witnessing firsthand the fact that a **16-year-old** **You** **Tuber** can deliver us **3X's** the traffic in a couple of days that some excellent traditional media coverage has over 5 months."

—Michael Fox, Co-Founder of Shoes of Prey

As I write this, nearly ten thousand people a month use Google to search the Internet for a church in Grand Rapids, Michigan.[3] How many are searching in your city? Will those searching find you? YouTube is the second largest search engine in the world (Practical Social Media University 2012), meaning people are searching for things on YouTube including information about churches, religion, and God.

Over three billion videos are viewed each day on YouTube. Over eight hundred million unique users visit YouTube each month ("Statistics"). That's a lot of people! Considering one of the primary goals of churches and ministries is to reach people, don't you think it would be a good idea to broadcast your message where people are? The answer seems obvious, but what about the objections?

Some ministers have wondered how to get on YouTube when they don't even own a camera. But they don't need one (I'll prove it later in the chapter). They wonder how they can afford YouTube's fees, but the service is free. They worry about questionable content, but I will show you some easy precautions to take to stay safe. Some people question, "Isn't social media just hype? Can you really get legitimate results?" I can personally attest that you can absolutely get legitimate results because my team and I have.

In 2010 I co-founded a nonprofit with my friend Jeff Moors called THiNK International to train the next generation of leaders and creatives to better reach people. So far we have released over one hundred training videos to pastors, leaders, interns, church planters, and missionaries from around the globe, and have gathered over a quarter million views on YouTube. If you do a YouTube search for "church media," a THiNK media video will likely be the first result, and a THiNK International video will be the second. We have had first-time guests visit my church in Las Vegas because of our presence and content on social media sites like YouTube (search "Las Vegas Church" on YouTube).

So how did we do it?

HOW YOUTUBE CAN EXTEND THE REACH OF YOUR CURRENT MARKETING AND OUTREACH EFFORTS

If used correctly, YouTube will bring about a multitude of benefits for your organization:

- Increased traffic to your main website or blog

- Another way for donors to give financially

- Free high-definition hosting for your videos

- Better search results for all your web content

- Ability to connect with people around the world

- A free platform to broadcast your message to the masses

- A place to promote your events and services online

- Massive integration with other social platforms

- A great way to build your organization's brand

- A way to get information to your network

However, when looking at all the benefits, it is important to also observe some pitfalls. The good news is that you can avoid them.

COMMON OBJECTIONS
TO CHURCHES USING YOUTUBE

There are a few things to be aware of when venturing onto YouTube. While they are not deal breakers, you should be prepared for them. Some of those issues include negative and distasteful comments, objectionable content, a look that is not as classy as other video sharing sights, and customization limitations. While these are all valid points, they should not keep churches and ministries off of this powerful platform.

I've been amazed by some of the negative comments we have received on our channels. When you participate in a community on the Internet, you don't get to choose who will be part of your community. You will need to develop thick skin and not take it personally when someone begins bashing you on the Internet. Did Jesus ever get negative comments? Of course, and so will you. YouTube gives you three options when it comes to comments—allow comments automatically, allow all comments with approval only, or don't allow comments. I choose to accept comments automatically and then I moderate them myself. This allows community to occur without me having to mediate 24/7, and the majority of comments are constructive. When I receive a comment I need to delete, there is a brief time before I remove it when others can see it. I think the smooth functioning of the community is worth this, but if you want to avoid the drama altogether, you can just select option three.

Is there objectionable content on YouTube? Yes. However, if you set up things correctly you will be protected. To weed out potentially objectionable content, I recommend you use YouTube's "Safety Mode." For your computers at home and at the office, this is a great way to keep your team and family safe. To enable this, log onto your YouTube account, scroll to the bottom of the page, and click "Safety Mode" from "off" to "on."

Additionally, if you want to embed a YouTube video in your blog or website, occasionally objectionable videos will appear in the sidebar. To avoid this you can use a free service called QuietTube (QuietTube.com) that will reveal only the video with no surrounding material.

While it may be true that other video sharing sights look better or have more customization than YouTube, consider two key points. First, YouTube is completely free. It used to have video length limitations and other constraints, but many of those have been changed. The fact that you can essentially upload an unlimited amount of video, even high-definition sixty-minute messages, for free is pretty astounding. Second, YouTube is where people are! YouTube trumps all other video sharing sites when it comes to the number of unique visitors. If our goal is to reach people, we need to navigate the pitfalls with wisdom and spread

God's love and redemption over this platform. So, what are you waiting for? Let's set your YouTube channel up and get your message out to the world!

GETTING STARTED WITH YOUTUBE: SETTING UP YOUR CHANNEL THE RIGHT WAY

Builders know that if the foundation is wrong, everything built on it will be wrong too. In the same way, it's important that you correctly set up your YouTube channel. There are multiple steps for this that will take some time, but the investment you make up front will pay off in the end if you stick to it.

1. Name your channel. You should put as much thought into naming your channel as you would for your website or anything else on the web. Your channel name will look like this: youtube.com/yourchannelname. Some good rules to remember are to keep it short, easy to remember, and containing your keywords. Avoid adding random numbers to your name if it's not available, like this: youtube.com/mychurch56678. Instead, try adding words like media or video to your account name, like this: youtube.com/mychurchmedia or mychurchvideo.

2. Thoroughly fill out all the information in "settings & profile." Under the settings tab, make sure to write a good title (this does not affect your channel name) and fill out your channel tags. If you have never figured out the top thirty keywords for your Internet marketing strategy, go to Google's Keyword Tool (https://adwords.google.com/select/KeywordToolExternal) and figure out your keywords. These words will become the words or tags you'll want to use in all social media where tags are an option. These tags are keywords used to help people find your channel. Make sure you take enough time to consider what your target audience is searching for, so that they can easily find you.

Under "Profile," add your name, style, website, and channel description. Make sure you also add your hometown and country. There are multiple other categories to fill out as well, which can help people find you when searching. However, in order to make your channel as clean and professional as possible, avoid too much text or clutter.

3. Thoroughly fill out all the information in the "Profile Setup" section. Sound redundant? It is. Your profile setup is actually in two places, so you'll want to make sure you fill out both. Here you can add a description (keep it short and to the point). If you're creating a channel for an organization, I would make sure gender and relationship is blank and your age is not displayed (it would be weird for your five-year-old church to be fifty-five and married).

4. Upload a profile picture. Get your church or ministries logo in a square format that is 600 x 600 pixels. Upload it as your profile picture. This size image can be used not only for YouTube but also for Twitter, Facebook, and any other social networks your organization is on. This aids in keeping clean and consistent branding across all platforms.

5. Customize your YouTube background. YouTube allows custom backgrounds that can include graphic design and images, giving your channel an even more unique personality. If you don't have the resources to create a YouTube background, you can at least change the color scheme. In your channel, under settings, you'll see an option to select a color right in YouTube. If you want to create a custom background, make its resolution 2000 x 2200 pixels. To see an example of how you can make your channel look customized for your ministry, take a look at the THiNK Intl. site here: http://www.youtube.com/thinkintl.

6. Modules, videos, and playlists. Lastly, you can control and move around what modules are viewable on your channel and how your videos look and play. Modules include the channel, comments, subscribers, and recent activity. You might want to turn most of these off to keep things as clean, simple, and professional as possible. Likewise, "Videos and Playlist" lets you customize what videos play on your channel. To watch a free video walkthrough of how to set up your channel, visit youtubeforchurches.com.

UPLOADING VIDEOS TO YOUR NEW CHANNEL: EVEN WITHOUT A CAMERA

Now that you have a YouTube channel, it's time to start uploading videos. If you already have a promo video for your church or ministry, you could upload that, or you could shoot a brand-new video if you have the necessary resources. But what if you don't have a video camera or don't want to be seen on camera?

Here are a few options:

1. **Check out animoto.com,** which is a user-friendly site that lets you create videos by uploading still images and video clips. You can add music and text, and it does all the work for you. There are free options as well as paid ones.

2. **If your laptop has a microphone,** or if you have a USB microphone, you can create a voice-over video inviting people to your church or promoting an event. Just write the script, record it on your computer, and add still images and text in free video editing software such as Windows Live Movie Maker for the PC or iMovie for the Mac.

3. **You can also use screen capture software** that allows you to record what you are doing on your computer desktop and lets you add narration. You can essentially create a video that explains how to get to your church with Google Maps or how to navigate your website, pointing out specific things that might interest users.

It is likely you have access to a video camera, even if it's cheap or just the video camera on your cell phone, so go for it! Shoot and then upload your first video to YouTube.

OPTIMIZE YOUR YOUTUBE VIDEOS FOR MASSIVE RESULTS

One of the biggest mistakes I see churches make over and over again is when they upload really great videos to their channels, videos they spent time, energy, and money on, but don't take the time to optimize them so they are actually seen. How you optimize your videos once you upload them is just as important as the video itself, if not more so.

Here is what to do every time you upload a video:

1. Give it a strategic title. The title of every one of your videos should be intentional and reverse engineered for your audience. Try to also find ways to include your keywords when you title your videos. Ultimately, you want your title to be interesting so people will actually want to click on it. Your first title may have your keywords in it, such as "Church—Grand Rapids, Michigan, Christian" but is lacking flow, interest, and readability. Consider this title instead: "Great church in Grand Rapids called [name of your church] invites you and your family this weekend." Your goal is not only to include keywords but also to create a good headline that people will want to click on.

2. Fully utilize the description. The first line of the description should contain your primary website URL. Make sure to always include "http://" before all URLs on YouTube. This makes them clickable and therefore easier for your viewer to get directly to your website from the link. The words you speak in your video are not searchable, but text in the description is, so don't hesitate to include lots of keyword-rich text every time. In some videos I have even included *all* of my notes from a seminar in the description area.

3. Be thorough and specific with your tags. When adding tags, make sure to include your selected keywords every time, as well as video-specific tags. Your selected keyword tags might include the name of your church, pastor, city, and general terms related to your niche. The video-specific tags might include the band name of the concert you're promoting, a specific sermon series title, or anything that only pertains to that video.

BORROW IDEAS FROM OTHERS WHO ARE SUCCEEDING ON YOUTUBE

When it comes to customizing your channel, creating videos, and writing titles and descriptions, don't hesitate to model your content after those who are already seeing great results. Feel free to go to youtube.com/thinkintl, our channel for THiNK International, or youtube.com/thechurchlvmedia, the main channel for my local church, and observe how I optimize videos. Then, just take the principles and apply them in your niche context.

THE FINAL STEP ONCE YOUR VIDEO IS ONLINE

Uploading your video to YouTube is just the first step. Your social media strategy should include the use of multiple platforms to share your video and get maximum exposure. Here's the sequence:

1. Upload and optimize your video.

2. Embed your video on your website or in a blog post.

3. Share your video on Twitter, Facebook, and Google+.

4. Send an email to your list that includes a link to your video.

5. Whatever your primary social media platforms are, make sure to always cross-promote your content across all of them (it's called "integrated marketing" because you are integrating all your resources in your distribution strategy). This is where you can get creative and experiment. You never know, maybe you will have the next viral video!

GENERAL THOUGHTS ABOUT
USING YOUTUBE AS A PLATFORM

It's important to know a couple other things about the YouTube community. YouTube is not just a video hosting website but is actually a social network and in fact, a real community. That means that there are two-way conversations taking place. You can leave comments, subscribe to peoples' channels, add friends, send messages, like or dislike videos, favorite videos, and even leave video comments. Just like there are social skills needed to succeed in our physical communities, the same is true for YouTube.

Make it your goal to subscribe to other YouTube channels relevant to your niche and area. Leave supportive comments and "like" other people's videos. Contribute to the conversations going on and add value to the community. In doing so, you will see your own channel and videos perform better as well! Colossians 4:5 says, "Be wise in the way you act toward outsiders; make the most of every opportunity." YouTube presents a huge opportunity for our churches and ministries to interact with outsiders, but it's important that we use wisdom when interacting with the community and while creating content.

PARTING WISDOM ABOUT GETTING STARTED

I have had people ask me, "What's the best way to get started on You-Tube?" My typical response is, "Just start." No doubt about it, it's hard learning new platforms and rules for new communities, but the quickest way to learn how to swim is to get in the water. Don't be afraid to make mistakes, because you will make a lot of them. Just learn from them and do better next time.

For those wanting comprehensive training on using YouTube for churches, ministries, and nonprofits, visit youtubeforchurches.com. There you will find free resources as well as my video course featuring step-by-step video walkthroughs and advanced tactics, techniques, and strategies. You can also visit thinkintl.tv for lots of free leadership and creative content for you and your team.

8

On #theFringe

"The world has changed. Mayberry went straight from the VCR to managing your life and your entertainment in the palm of your hand with an iPhone in seconds flat. We need to be able to speak intelligently into the conversation as Christians."

—John Voelz

If I were to list every social media networking site or platform that exists, I'd be writing forever. When it comes to sharing with you, I felt it best to narrow the field to just four of the top platforms that ministry leaders are currently using. There are certainly others that church leaders find very user-friendly and may even use daily, but those didn't make my list. With that said, I feel like I should at least acknowledge some of the platforms that fall into this category.

Wikis: Wikis are websites that allow the public to contribute or edit content. These sites are great for collaboration, such as creating a large document or project plan with a team in several offices. A wiki can be as private or as open as the people who create it want it to be. The most famous wiki is Wikipedia, an online encyclopedia that was started in 2001. It now has over 2.5 million articles in English alone. Wikipedia is a trusted source. As mentioned in another chapter, studies have shown Wikipedia to have a very high degree of accuracy.

Flickr: Flickr is the world's leading photo management and online sharing application. This platform allows people to share their photos with the world and also helps you organize your pictures and videos. If you have a digital camera, it can be pretty easy to become overwhelmed with the number of pictures you take. With Flickr, you can even give your friends and family permission to organize your materials and add their own comments.

LinkedIn: A growing professional social network with over 120 million members worldwide. This online profile represents your experience (education, work, references, etc.). It's sort of an online résumé site. You can make connections with people you know and trust, and it helps you become more productive in your ministry. One strength of the site is that you can find resources by simply sharing your need with contacts through the site.

Just through a search of terms on LinkedIn you might find a person in your network who can meet your need. For example, let's say I wanted to help get more traffic to my website and rank a little higher in Google's search. I would probably attempt to locate someone who has experience with SEO. If I entered "SEO" in the search on Linkedin, I would find that ClickFinders.com, a Search Engine Optimization company, was in my network. I can quickly reach them through my contacts.

> "SOCIAL MEDIA, IT TURNS OUT, ISN'T ABOUT AGGREGATING AUDIENCES SO YOU CAN YELL AT THEM ABOUT THE JUNK YOU WANT TO SELL. SOCIAL MEDIA, IN FACT, IS A BASIC HUMAN NEED, REVEALED DIGITALLY ONLINE. WE WANT TO BE CONNECTED, TO MAKE A DIFFERENCE, TO MATTER, TO BE MISSED. WE WANT TO BELONG, AND YES, WE WANT TO BE LED."
> —SETH GODIN

Social bookmarking: Social bookmarking is a method for Internet users to organize, store, manage, and search for bookmarks of resources online. Instead of saving or bookmarking articles to your web browser, social bookmarking allows you to post and share them on such sites as Digg, StumbleUpon, and Delicious. Because your bookmarks are web-based, it means they are also social and can be shared with your friends or followers. Bloggers frequently attach a bookmark to selected posts to share them and drive traffic to those sites.

Google+: Google+ is a social networking site that operates very much like Facebook. Users can post status updates, share links, pictures, videos, and more. Each Google+ profile centers around the "stream," which is essentially the same thing as Facebook's News Feed, where all of your info and updates from your friends, family, and acquaintances are rounded up and constantly updated. Much like the way Twitter operates, on Google+ I can follow you and you don't have to follow me. And like Facebook, with the easy share buttons and threaded conversations, the entire network can come into contact with every post you share. The stream is joined by four core elements—Circles, Hangouts, Huddle, and Sparks. As of this writing, Google+ has struggled to attract the same audience as Facebook. But because it comes from Google—a company known for their innovation on the Internet—it's worth knowing about and keeping tabs on.

MyYearbook: MyYearbook is another social networking site created to help people connect with old friends and make new ones. This site has over thirty-three million users who exchange messages, pictures, and play social games. The creators of the site incorporated social games tied together by a single virtual currency called "lunch money." As a user you can earn the money by playing games, wagering in battle, and even spend your lunch money by donating to a social cause.

MySpace: What is MySpace? Even though MySpace isn't as widely accepted (or used) by ministry leaders today, the popular social networking site, co-owned by pop star Justin Timberlake, still has over eighty million users and is listed among the top five social networking sites of all time. The site is still favored by some over Facebook because of the ability to customize profiles. The applications are similar to current Facebook applications, including chat, messages, and online games. While Facebook has far eclipsed MySpace as the general public's social network of choice, MySpace remains core to some groups—such as singers and musicians. Not only might some members of your church use MySpace to post new songs, it's a key place to locate anyone involved with Christian music.

Instagram: Between 2010 and 2011, this free, mobile, photo-based social network grew from one to fifteen million members (Digital Mom Blog 2012). I personally use this mobile app frequently and enjoy all the creative filters available for sharing my photos. It won't be long before Instagram video is a major social outlet as well.

Ning: Ning is an online platform that was created for people and organizations to create custom social networks. Ning offers its users the opportunity to create a community website with customization to their liking. Users can change the appearance, feel, and feature photos, videos, forums, blogs, and integrate other social networks such as Facebook, Twitter, and Google.

Ustream: This online platform allows you to live stream (video) your events, services, and messages online so that members and nonmembers can view your service when they cannot be there in person. The nice thing about this platform is that you can add the Ustream Facebook application so that you can stream your events through your Facebook page too!

Podcasts: A podcast is basically a nonstreamed webcast that is a series of digital media files, whether audio or video, that can be categorized, typically released as episodes, and are available and often downloaded through web syndication. Many churches use these to broadcast their sermons to users worldwide.

Even though this isn't an exhaustive listing, I've provided information on many social networks and social mediums that exist today. Here's the thing: social media platforms will come and go. What is important is that you understand what is available to you and that you see the endless possibilities for building a healthy virtual community where you reach out to others and share your life with them.

9

#BabySteps

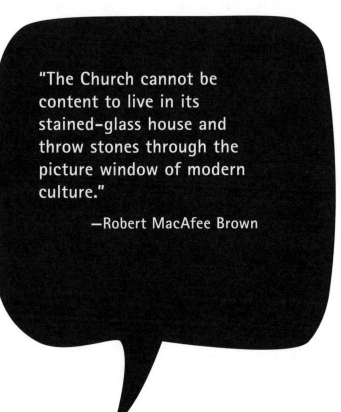

"The Church cannot be content to live in its stained-glass house and throw stones through the picture window of modern culture."

—Robert MacAfee Brown

So you're ready to dive in but aren't quite sure you'd like to swim in the deep end just yet. You want to take some baby steps first . . . get your feet wet. You might also still have some reservations about taking the plunge because of some things you've heard about social media. In this chapter I'll attempt to clear some of this up for you and I'll also share some helpful tips on how you can start out small.

First, let me share with you some things that I hear quite often but are things that are untrue about social media. These are things that are commonly spoken as "truth" but they aren't; we might call them "myths."

MYTHS AND MYTH-BUSTERS

MYTH 1: If I create it, people will immediately follow. If you don't give people a reason to come back to your site every day, it won't be long before they forget about you. Content plus consistency equals readership. Content really is king, and making sure you always have new content is key. It also helps to integrate your different online spaces, like a blog and a Facebook page, for example, to help maximize the visibility of your content.

MYTH 2: We need to be on every platform. Many churches and organizations think that in order to be relevant, they must be on every platform. There are some people who maximize only one space, one social media platform, and they do it really well. Sure, you want to stay ahead of the curve and remain relevant, but you also want to make sure you're going where your audience is and having meaning-ful conversations. In some cases, that does mean having a presence on most social media outlets. But in other cases, especially where you have limited time and resources, it may mean that you narrow the field to just a couple of platforms.

For example, let's say your focus is teenagers. You might find that the students are very active on Facebook but they don't really use Twitter. In this particular case, it does not make sense for you to devote time to maximizing your Twitter presence, especially if it's going to take away from your Facebook strategies.

From a branding perspective it would make sense, however, to go ahead and create a Twitter account before someone else gets the one you want. This way, just in case your students start using Twitter—or whatever the next big social media thing is tomorrow—you'll be ready to act.

MYTH 3: If they are not talking to me, I can tune out. Listening to what people are saying online is a great opportunity to engage people in conversations, meet other people's immediate felt needs, and pos-sibly even grow your audience. Companies have started doing this by extending their customer service to Twitter. Recently a friend of mine had a complaint about a company, so he tweeted about it. Within one hour the company he was talking about on Twitter replied to his tweet, and then after an exchange of his contact information, they called him personally to follow up and make things right.

I did a quick search on Twitter (search.Twitter.com) for the phrase "I hate God" and found over a dozen people who made that statement today alone. Doing something like this can be an easy way to find someone who may be willing to have a pretty deep conversation. Even if people are not talking to you (or about you), don't tune out. There's a world of opportunity to make an impact.

MYTH 4: Social media makes a great soapbox. Platforms like your blog, Twitter, and Facebook fan page shouldn't be treated like your personal soapbox where you try to blast everyone in the hopes of drowning out everybody else. And believe me, some people use it for this purpose. If you use your social media platforms to do this, it will probably make you more enemies than friends and result in people unfollowing you. A good rule is to treat your online friends like your offline friends. Play nice. Ask questions. Respond to comments and strive to engage in meaningful conversations with people online.

Next, let's talk about some things you can do to start small. I'd like to offer you five tips that will help you get started in social media.

5 TIPS FOR GETTING STARTED

1. Start reading. As mentioned in the earlier chapters, one of the things you need to do is to start reading blogs, listening to the conversation on Facebook and Twitter, and start watching YouTube videos.

2. Follow others. Don't just click "follow" or "subscribe" to a feed, but actually follow people. Chances are that you will learn a lot from listening in and even engaging in conversation through replies and commenting.

3. Don't be afraid to ask questions. I have conversations with people each week and ask questions. It doesn't matter where you are now as much as what steps you are taking to get to where you want to be. Be proactive.

4. See what works for you. Most likely you won't like every social media platform equally. You will get the most enjoyment out of one, while still utilizing the others. For instance, my favorite platform is Twitter. I like the brevity and the instant response I can get from my audience. Experiment around on each platform and see what works for you.

10

#Lean_In_

"While your message as a follower of Christ is grace, hope and healing, there's a power that works equally hard online (and off-line) to cancel out your message by generating a perpetual flow of despair, hate, and evil."

— @StickyJesus

Years ago when one of my mentors wanted to share something of significance with me he would often say, "Now lean in and listen." It meant that his words, often his parting words, were about to be spoken and he wanted my undivided attention. This chapter is dedicated to that: some parting words.

TEMPTATION ONLINE

Earlier in this book, I mentioned reasons that ministry leaders stay away from social media. One reason I did not mention is that some leaders are trying to avoid the temptation they may face online. Just last week I heard a horrible story about a ministry leader who had to step down from his position in ministry because he made some poor choices, and now he's fighting for his marriage. It is true that you may face temptation online because of your use of the platforms outlined in this book. But just as you face temptations otherwise, you must recognize that we have an enemy in this world, and we have an advocate. You must be prepared for the enemy and rely on help from the advocate. I love what 1 John 4:4 says, "The one who is in you is greater than the one who is in the world."

If you have a problem controlling your thoughts, eyes, or flesh because of the Internet surfing that you do online already, don't expect to be free from it as you engage in conversations and community through social media.

Here are some tips to help you with boundaries as you are on social networks:

Friending: You may choose to restrict access on your Facebook page to only people that you really know. You can switch your privacy settings to "friends only."

Pictures: Be careful of the pictures you post on your account(s). Make sure your pictures are modest and also be aware that pictures can be digitally modified.

Vacations or business trips: Many church leaders I know will be careful not to mention when they are out of town, whether on vacation or business, for the safety of their families. You might also consider this when you are taking time away.

Meeting publicly: I've heard that a large number of virtual friends who have been connected for more than a year will eventually meet in person. If that is true, you should be careful when choosing to meet publicly. You might consider taking a friend with you. It might be wise to share the details about the person you are meeting with several people, including your family.

Conversations with members of the opposite sex: If you are married and are using social media, be careful of your conversations with anyone of the opposite sex. You might not find certain things inappropriate, but the question to ask is whether others might find them inappropriate. If you are single, you might also be careful of divulging too much private information.

Rest: Being "connected" online can be addictive for many people. Many ministry leaders find it hard to detach from their social networks. I'd encourage you to have some accountability with this. Take breaks when you need to and occasionally unplug from social media altogether when you need to focus.

Word choice: Be careful to choose your words before you send an update from any social media platform. Realize that your updates are being pushed to all followers and subscribers who are a part of your virtual community. I've seen too many times where an argument breaks out on Twitter or Facebook (or even in the comments fields of a YouTube account or blog) and things get really messy. Make sure you remember that these words are public. If you wouldn't be comfortable with what you post being plastered up on a billboard for everyone to see, chances are you shouldn't be posting it online.

SHARE WHAT YOU'VE BEEN GIVEN

I heard an interview recently where Charlene Li, author of *Open Leadership,* was sharing about social media. She stated, "What has happened over the last three years is that we now have a culture of sharing that didn't exist three years ago. Now we think and act very differently because of these technologies. The societal change that has happened is that we share more" (Li).

Dear God, let that continue. Amen.

Why is it that when we are young it is so common to share with others but as we get older we lose that ability? I was excited to hear that there is a shift taking place in our culture. I've seen this change in many places and I hope to see it more. Whether you have a blog, Twitter, Facebook, YouTube account, or whatever, make sure you adopt a philosophy of sharing. Here are a few ways, some I've mentioned already, that are great ways of sharing in the social media environment.

1. Share link love. One of the things that I really like to do is to point people to things that I recommend. I most often do this on my Twitter account. Provide links to things that you find enjoyable or that may be of particular interest to others who follow you. I must warn you, though—following me on Twitter may be a bit like drinking through a fire hose. I like to share links.

2. Share your network. Networking is one thing that makes me tick. I love connecting people to others who can help them. When you don't have the resources to help someone yourself, you can always be the middleman who connects them. Just last week I saw a tweet from someone who was in desperate need of a graphic designer. They put out a Twitter plea for help and I stepped in and connected them with a friend of mine who is a great artist. This kind of opportunity seems to present itself each week; we just have to be looking!

3. Share your knowledge. I believe that everyone has something that he or she is good at. It's important to not take this for granted but to use your life to help others around you. This also applies to social media. Share what you know. You'll be surprised at how fulfilling it is to share the knowledge.

4. Share your compassion. One reason I'm partial to Twitter (even though I see this present on other platforms as well) is because I see people sharing their concern and having compassion for others. Yes, there are a lot of cruel people on these platforms too, but it makes me feel good to see people praying for others, sharing scriptures, and sharing encouragement in their tweets.

DON'T DROP THE "SOCIAL" FROM SOCIAL MEDIA

I'm amazed at how many people literally seem to drop the word "social" from social media. I see bloggers who close their comments field and people on Twitter who never engage with their followers but rather "push" or promote their content instead. It's important we understand the importance of virtual community.

1. Responding to followers. One rule of thumb I think everyone needs to abide by when it comes to social media is the importance of replying and responding to followers or subscribers. I realize that once you have reached a pretty large following it's harder to manage, but attempting to engage with your community is vital. It does my heart good to see popular church leaders who are replying to their readers' comments on their blogs or being an active participant in their comment thread on Facebook.

One of my favorite bloggers decided nearly two years ago to close the comments on his blog because he was getting some anonymous comments that were not kind. I definitely understand this as I have sometimes received the same treatment on my blog, but I really missed being able to interact with him and be a part of the community. Eventually I drafted an email to him and pleaded with him to open the comments again. I'm proud to say after a few days he honored my request and opened his comments again.

2. Be authentic. Your readers will really appreciate this one. I realize that you can't respond or reply to every person who contacts you on your social media platforms, but I urge you to at least share on a personal level. It's a great way to help people who subscribe to your feed to connect with you.

3. Flattery will get you everywhere. As you grow your audience, you may not be able to reply to folks personally as often as you like but you can at least retweet them when appropriate. I've seen celebrities and major corporations do this. When they are tweeted by a fan or someone that says something particularly positive about them, they will often retweet it. Who doesn't like getting attention like that? I'd encourage you to follow that same principle. Share love, even when you can't necessarily provide your undivided attention.

11

Twenty Examples, #Twenty_Stories

Shaun King—Twit Change, blogger, church planter, philanthropist
www.shauninthecity.com
Twitter.com/shaunking

Shaun King, former pastor of Courageous Church in Atlanta, Georgia, sure knows how to use social media. In a recent conversation with Shaun I asked him what social media meant to him. He replied, "Social media is central to my life. Some of my best friends are Twitter friends. They aren't fake. They're real. Social media makes the world so much smaller and makes doing good and advocating for people so much easier. I have people who I've raised millions of dollars with (and for) that I've never met face-to-face—our relationships are virtual and for me that's OK."

It seems like the 2010 earthquake in Haiti sent shockwaves to Shaun's soul. Ever since that natural disaster, Shaun has been on a mission to start a revolution of good. Shaun saw so many people without a home that he launched a website (ahomeinhaiti.org) dedicated to raising funds to provide tents to homeless persons. His good works didn't stop there.

King saw the growing need among the Haitian people, particularly children with disabilities. He had an idea for a charity auction in which he would partner with celebrities to raise money for a cause. Soon after, TwitChange.com was born. TwitChange is the first-ever celebrity tweet auction that allowed fans of nearly two hundred celebrities to bid on three things: to be followed by their favorite celebrity on Twitter, retweeted, or mentioned by them in a special tweet. Funds raised through the event would be used to construct The Miriam Center in Haiti, which would house, educate, and spiritually support children with cerebral palsy, severe autism, and other challenges. After the ten-day auction, over eleven thousand bids had been placed and TwitChange. com received more than twenty-six million hits, raised over a million dollars, and received national media attention (Selders 2011).

Shaun is currently working on his newest project called "Hopemob." Shaun says, "I honestly think Hopemob is going to become the most revolutionary generosity platform in the world. This platform," he says, "will be all about meeting the emergency needs of people around the world."

Life in Student Ministry with Tim Schmoyer
www.studentministry.org
www.onlinemissionstrip.com

In 2009 my friend Tim Schmoyer came up with a great idea. He became a bit discontented with outreach events and had an idea for a missions trip that would leverage media. He explained, "The Internet has never made it so easy to share Christ with those all over the world! Teenagers spend a crazy amount of hours talking with friends on Facebook, MySpace, YouTube, online role-playing games, and other such social hangouts online about things that don't really matter in light of eternity. So let's train them to share their faith and push them to do it online" (Schmoyer). Tim soon created an "Online Missions Trip," a two-week campaign to empower students to use social media to share Christ with their friends who don't yet know him.

Next he developed a little bit of structure, did some pre-missions trip planning, and put together some resources for students as well. He then developed a website, www.onlinemissionstrip.com, and shared that idea with youth workers around the globe. In my recent phone conversation with Tim, he said that according to his site statistics, over three thousand people participated in the first-ever online missions trip and the only continent that did not participate in some way was Antarctica.

Tim also developed a website dedicated to answering questions that ministry leaders have, which you can access at www.ministryquestions.com.

LifeChurch.tv—YouVersion
LifeChurch, Edmond, Oklahoma
Craig Groeschel, senior pastor
www.lifechurch.tv
swerve.lifechurch.tv

LifeChurch.tv is run by LifeChurch in Edmond, Oklahoma, but has a global reach. The one thing that LifeChurch is best known for is their generosity. Their open.lifechurch.tv site is a website devoted to re-sourcing churches and church leaders around the world with free, downloadable resources.

Since its launch in 1996, LifeChurch's purpose has been to lead people to become fully devoted followers of Christ. In doing so, the church has looked for new ways to help people connect the Bible to their daily lives. The methods have changed over the years as they have incorporated various technologies and strategies, but at the core their focus remains on relevancy as they strive to demonstrate and teach people how God's Word relates to everyone—no matter where they are in life. One remarkable thing about LifeChurch.tv is their innovative nature. YouVersion is a great example of their innovative nature. Developers had expected around seventy thousand people to sign up (and download) the app in the first year. Instead, the app was downloaded by over eighty thousand people in the first three days alone!

Today, more than nineteen million users have downloaded the Bible app to their phone or mobile device. The app also allows you to bookmark scriptures and share your reading with friends via social networks.

Bobby Gruenewald, the creator of the app, told CBN news earlier this year, "With the Bible now as close as your phone, I'm hopeful this new technology will help reverse the trend of less Bible reading. My perspective is not that we can just turn the tide a bit on that trend, but I actually believe it's possible that we can have the most Bible-engaged generation in history" (Griffith 2011). Gruenewald believes that the app could reach nearly a half billion people before all is said and done. LifeChurch has even expanded their staff to help manage the demand of the more than nineteen million users worldwide.

Mark Driscoll, senior pastor
Mars Hill Church, Seattle, Washington
www.marshillchurch.org
www.theresurgence.com/blog

Driscoll was named one of the 25 Most Influential Pastors of the Past 25 Years by *Preaching* magazine, and his sermons are consistently number 1 on iTunes each week for Religion & Spirituality, with millions of downloads each year. I had to highlight Mark Driscoll in this book because he is one of the most notable pastors in America who is using technology to its fullest potential.

A *USA Today* article, "Pastors Are Flocking to Facebook, Twitter," featured Seattle-based Mars Hill Church. With more than ten thousand members at (then) nine locations, the church is a robust user of Facebook, Twitter, and YouTube, church spokesman Nick Bogardus says. At its best, social media "opens an opportunity to build a real relationship" (Revehl 2010).

As an example, he mentions a single mother and first-time church visitor who posted a thank-you for the sermon on Facebook the following Monday. "Pastor Mark followed up with a note to her saying, 'Please find me or another minister the next time you visit, so we can get better acquainted,'" Bogardus says (Revehl 2010).

So how is Mars Hill using technology and the web to reach people? Driscoll says,

Our podcasts and MP3s (primarily sermons along with some worship music) are now over a million downloads per year. We recently launched vodcasts (downloadable videos delivered to you automatically), and they debuted at number one in the iTunes spirituality section, which was cool. Under Mars Hill's TheResurgence.com, there are tens of thousands of pages of free missional theology, including articles and book reviews, along with blogs, podcasts, and vodcasts of sermons, conferences, and classroom messages. The site features a lot of free training from me and other well-known Christian leaders for pastors around the world. We are also constantly developing our church site and our church-planting site. Most of what we do technologically—to be honest—has virtually nothing to do with me. I produce a mountain of content each year and have been blessed by some godly, helpful tech folks who get it out to the world. Without them, I am just yet another peculiar guy with a lot of Word documents on his computer. In the future, we will use whatever technology trend emerges. I hope we will be one of the first to use it for the gospel of Jesus to reach as many people as possible through what Paul called "all methods available." (Revehl 2010)

THiNK International—Going Viral
Sean Cannell, co-founder
www.thinkintl.tv

THiNK International was founded by Jeff Moors and Sean Cannell as a solution to an increasingly irrelevant church. In July of 2010 they set off to develop something that would bring hope, spark creativity, and empower ministries, churches, and organizations around the world to reach people.

Together, Jeff and Sean form an unreal team that has the ability make stuff happen. They are students of the church and of culture with a heart to reach people. This makes them incredibly effective when it comes to generating ideas that create results. Being able to see future trends before they materialize, Jeff and Sean stay ahead of the game. They want leaders to think bigger, faster, more creatively, and well, just different from the average person.

THiNK offers training to church leaders in preaching, teaching, creativity, and media (among others). Sean Cannell (who helped write the chapter on YouTube), serves as the director of communications for the Church at South Las Vegas. Sean's passion for helping ministries get on YouTube is exciting. He recently launched a site devoted to helping train others in how to launch their ministries on YouTube, which you can visit at www.youtubeforchurches.com.

Matt McKee, CEO
ROAR—A Mobile App Company
www.mattmckee.me
www.ROAR.pro

Matt McKee is an entrepreneur to his core. He's started or helped start companies for many years. He oozes creativity and enjoys sharing ideas and resources with others. His latest company is ROAR, which creates iPhone and Android apps for nonprofits and those that serve nonprofits.

Did you know that the number 1 app on iPhones and Android is Facebook? Social media has been growing at a fast pace, but McKee says that, "Since the birth of the smartphone, conversations and interaction among people has been taken to a new level." He says, "I find it interesting that people don't sweat paying 30 bucks a month for a mobile phone data package to just stay connected online and to talk with their friends."

McKee founded his company to provide churches and organizations with mobile apps for their organization's social media when he saw that churches needed help leveraging social media for ministry. Why should church leaders take an interest in a mobile app?

"I think the local church is the prime spot for a local social network," he said. "Your church members want to share prayer requests, want to be up-to-date on information, and want to show their friend at work what exciting things are going on at their church. They want to share the mission, vision, and values with their friends and co-workers and having that in their pocket is great. I believe the best way to do that is through a mobile app" (personal interview, December 2011).

@TwitterStories
#TwitterStories
stories.Twitter.com

Recently I ran across a website developed to collect stories of how Twitter has changed lives. Here are some of those stories:

Bookstore Saved

Aaron Durand's mother ran an independent bookstore in Portland, Oregon. The bookstore was about to go out of business until Aaron sent a plea out on Twitter. He offered to buy a burrito for anyone who bought $50 worth of books during the holidays. His single tweet was retweeted over and over again and the bookstore went on to have the best holiday season ever and is still thriving to this day ("Aaron Durand saved his Mom's bookstore with a Tweet," 2008).

African Courts Opened

Dr. Willy M. Mutunga has given his life to deepening the democratic practices in Africa's court systems. After he was appointed to the Supreme Court in June 2011, he became the very first African Chief Justice to use Twitter in the courts ("Dr. Willy Mutunga opened the African courts to direct communication through Twitter," 2011).

Two People Rescued

A TV news anchor, Okan Bayulgen, used Twitter to send along emergency information when a 7.2 magnitude earthquake struck Turkey. One of his followers sent him an address where people were still trapped beneath the rubble. Relief workers were immediately dispatched and the two people were rescued within two hours ("Okan Bayulgen and Akut saved two people trapped by the earthquake in Turkey," 2011).

Reunited with Daughter

Underheard, a charity created to help the homeless, provides prepaid cellphones to those in need. The charity helped Daniel Morales obtain a phone and develop a Twitter account, too. He got the idea that he could use Twitter to find his daughter, Sarah Rivera. He posted his phone number, Sarah's name, and a photo of her. The message spread and just two days later they met in Bryant Park ("Daniel Morales reunites with his daughter after 11 years," 2011).

Got a Kidney

Chris Strouth lived with a kidney disease for over three years and was in desperate need of a transplant. He turned to Twitter and messaged, "I need a kidney." Within a few days, nineteen people replied to his tweet to find out if they might be a match for him. Pretty soon after some testing and a positive match, the surgery was done and Strouth was on his road to recovery ("Chris Strouth tweeted . . . ," 2009).

Gained a Voice

For nearly three decades, movie critic Roger Ebert shared his powerful opinions of cinema with the world, but in 2006, after complications from cancer surgery, he was left without the ability to speak. In addition to his printed column, his books, and his blog, Ebert now tweets. He gained a voice through social media ("Gained a voice," 2011).

Orangepedia
Orange | ReThink Group
www.whatisorange.org
www.rethinkgroup.com

Orange exists to provide vision, passion, and resources to children's and students' ministers. The organization conducts an annual tour across the country to meet with church leaders in small environments to answer questions and provide resources and support to these next-generation leaders. The support doesn't stop there, because Orange really seeks to leverage social media to help equip leaders too. The Orange Tour has its own blog that serves as an online hub for information relating to the tour. Check it out at blog.orangetour.org.

Perhaps one of the best wiki pages that I've seen in the church community belongs to Orange. Orange realized there was a growing need for a place for their leaders or "specialists" online, so they created Orangepedia, a wiki dedicated to serving them. This website allows users to upload articles and allows leaders to share their ideas too.

Orange also leverages other social media platforms, including blogs, Facebook, YouTube, and Twitter. Their Facebook page receives over two hundred thousand impressions each month, and their blog can be accessed directly at www.whatisorange.org or through Facebook. Orange also created a mobile app for their leaders, which is accessed by over ten thousand people each month.

Northland Church, Central Florida
Joel Hunter, senior pastor
www.northlandchurch.net

Northland Church in Longwood, Florida, is a great example of a church that is using Facebook to engage people in conversations around the world. The church, made up of over fifteen thousand attenders, has over four thousand people who attend their service weekly but have never set foot inside the facility! The church now streams at least five services online and made the jump to Facebook, where you can watch their services live.

Pastor Hunter remembers,

> We had grown big enough to become a society within a society. If we had wanted to just do the traditional things to accommodate growth (i.e., be in perennial building campaigns, keep motivating people to live as much of their lives at the church building as possible), then we could probably have kept growing. But growing what? Another mega church? We would be promoting the unspoken message that our own congregation was more important to us than other congregations and ministries, and furthering the Western mentality of the rugged individualism of a church while ignoring the larger community life of the global Church—a philosophy that is neither biblical nor appropriate.

The solution? Northland would construct a new church building that would serve as a distribution point rather than a destination (Northland Church, 2012).

Completed in August 2007, Northland's $42 million facility in Longwood, Florida, was built for both the local congregation and those who worship concurrently at other locations. The new facilities offer plenty of room—more than 160,000 square feet of space. However, the intent was never to see how many people could fit under one roof; it was to facilitate ministry worldwide with other believers. The facility features state-of-the-art technology with two-way interconnectivity that provides unlimited seating for worshipers . . . virtually (Northland Church 2012).

Westwinds Community Church, Jackson, Michigan
John Voelz and David McDonald, pastors
johnvoelzblog.blogspot.com
www.westwinds.org

In early 2009, John Voelz and David McDonald, the two senior pastors at Westwinds Community Church in Jackson, Michigan, spent nearly two weeks educating their congregation on how to use Twitter. They held training sessions in which they encouraged people to bring their laptops and their smartphones. They even increased the wireless bandwidth in the auditorium. Voelz told me that they have "Twitter Sundays" and encourage people to tweet to their followers during services. They even have a running Twitter feed displayed for congregants on projection screens. Westwinds Church was featured in *Time Magazine* in May of 2009 highlighting how they leverage Twitter (and technology) in church.

At Westwinds, people tweet questions about the sermon that the pastors will answer later, or that will spur other Twitter users in attendance to offer insight. Some even use their Twitter as a note-taking tool during the sermon. Voelz told me he gets no less than five emails, Facebook messages, or phone calls each week from people asking how they can launch Twitter within their church. Among the questions he gets asked is: How do you rig the screen so people can read the tweets? What is the overall reaction of the congregants at your church? Got any tips to help me persuade my church leadership that we should do this?

Voelz explains, "I am not surprised at all at the mixed reactions. As with anything new, some will be early adopters, some will love it, some will hate it, some won't care . . . and, they are all entitled to their opinion. We are just grateful to be in a place where this kind of thing is expected. We will try crazy things. We will go out on a limb. We will even fail. What a kick."

Some of the positive responses to the church's experiment?
"I felt like part of what was happening."
"I felt part of the community."
"I felt like a leader."
"I felt like it was about more than just me."

Carlos Whittaker, worship artist, blogger
www.ragamuffinsoul.com

Carlos Whittaker is an artist, pastor, thinker, experience architect, and web 2.0 junkie . . . or so his blog says. Carlos was at Sandals Church in Riverside, California, where he served for ten years as the pastor of worship and creative arts. Sandals Church is an authentic community of believers whose goal is to be real with themselves, others, and God. He has a passion for leading the church into a relational worship experience each and every Sunday.

In August of 2007, Carlos and his family made the move from Southern California to Atlanta, Georgia. Carlos became the director of service programming at Buckhead Church, which is one of the three North Point Community Church campuses. He oversaw all the Sunday adult experience and design. He directly oversaw all areas of production, creative, video, music, and programming at Buckhead. He also sat on the creative sermon planning team for Andy Stanley.

Early last year, Whittaker signed a record deal with Integrity Music to pursue a recording career. The thing is, Carlos isn't your typical worship artist. If you visit his popular blog, www.ragamuffinsoul.com, you'll soon find that out. Recently I asked a number of church leaders who they would name as someone who really understood what leveraging social media was all about and one name kept coming up over and over again—Carlos Whittaker. He gets it. If you don't believe me, follow him through his Twitter feed, blog, or YouTube channel for a brief time and you'll see what kind of virtual community he is building.

Pete Wilson, lead pastor
Cross Point Church, Nashville, Tennessee
www.withoutwax.tv
www.crosspoint.tv

Pete Wilson is the founding and senior pastor of Cross Point Church in Nashville, Tennessee. This is the second church he has planted in the last seven years. Cross Point has grown over the last eight years to one church with five different locations.

Pete doesn't just minister to the community at Cross Point, though—he has a growing virtual community that he has built through his personal blog, www.withoutwax.tv, and through his Twitter presence. Many pastors choose to have a blog to interact with the people in their congregations. There is nothing wrong with this at all. Pete blogs not only for the purpose of connecting with those who are a part of his church family but also to engage with those who aren't part of Cross Point Church. His blog is currently one of the most widely read pastors' blogs on the Internet.

I got the chance to ask Pete a few questions about his experience with social media.

TC: *What has been the greatest benefit for you, as you see it, to blogging as a pastor?*

PW: I think the greatest benefit to me is allowing to have a place where I'm not just a "talking head." I love the blog because it's a place where people can ask questions and interact unlike my Sunday morning message. The interaction has sharpened me in so many different ways.

TC: *Would you encourage other pastors and church leaders to blog?*

PW: I would definitely encourage other pastors to blog. Here are a couple reasons why:

Communication. Your blog is a great place to keep your people informed on what's going at your church. You can reinforce vision, challenge your community, and keep them in the loop all at the same time. I guarantee you they'll read your blog more intently than they read your Sunday bulletin.

Community. It's amazing how people feel connected to the day-to-day happenings of your life when you blog. You can share family stories and updates that don't fit into Sunday messages.

Willow Creek Church Association—Leadership Segment
Bill Hybels, senior pastor
Hanna Koenig, marketing manager
www.Twitter.com/hannaksays

Willow Creek Community Church was started back in 1972 and was just a dream of Pastor Bill Hybels. Today, more than twenty thousand people worship at one of Willow Creek's six regional campuses each weekend. Part of Willow's ministry to growing leaders around the world is through the Willow Creek Leadership Summit, which is attended by thousands of church leaders each year, thanks to the simulcast sites across the nation. Through social media they are able to share the conference with more than just those who attend the Summit. Hanna Koenig, the marketing manager of the Leadership segment at Willow, shared with me how the Summit leverages social media to bring this important event to so many church leaders each year.

"The Willow Creek Association really seeks to serve church leaders and over the past year, we've made an intentional effort to make sure that the voices on our blog have been from more than just our staff and leaders. We've been working to find ways to connect leaders to leaders," she says.

"With that in mind, we invited a team of bloggers to the Summit to attend by watching it backstage and tweeting/blogging throughout the event. We wanted to model being in relationship and that the Summit is so much more than just our team tweeting and posting." Hannah observed, "The bloggers had access to backstage and were able to interview speakers and take photos. I think it was successful; however, we have things that we learned along the way. Like, next year, we'll make sure we have bloggers who are in various host sites, not just the main campus. In retrospect, I'm glad we did this because it gave us a way to build some incredible relationships, giving us an opportunity to share the Summit online.

"In addition, having a strong social media presence during the event. This past year having that presence allowed us the opportunity to share Bill Hybels addressing a last-minute change of speakers when a major presenter pulled out. Because of our use of Twitter almost every speaker was trending (around the world) during their session. In the past year, our team has been working to use social media in an integrated way. What happened at the Summit was part of our value for connecting the online and off-line in valuable ways" ("Join the Impact Movement").

Westside Family Church, Lenexa, Kansas
www.westsidefamilychurch.com

I first heard about Westside Family Church because of their YouTube channel. Westside posts videos that range from sermons to funny clips to leadership training sessions provided by the staff. Their church is learning to leverage social media in some pretty amazing ways. Their main church website alone is pretty slick.

The Westside family is people who are not content to just "do church" but who are becoming a shining light of healing love in their community and world. Recently the church developed a campaign called "IMPACT," which is described as a fresh, God-sized vision to free people to follow Jesus by sharing the gospel, loving orphans, and breaking chains of poverty, injustice, disease, and illiteracy. IMPACT focuses on six critical areas of human need: J.O.S.E.P.H. (Justice, Orphans, Spiritual Movement, Education, Poverty, and Health).

In an effort to get IMPACT off the ground, the church turned to media, which included the development of a website (www.wfcimpact.com) and the use of social media networks, like Facebook (WFC).

Granger Community Church—Granger, Indiana
Mark Beeson, senior pastor
www.gccwired.com

In November 1986 Mark Beeson and his wife, Sheila, moved—against all popular advice and counsel—to Granger, Indiana, with their young children. They didn't have extended family or friends waiting for them, just a vision to start a different kind of church. They didn't have all the answers to the questions people were asking. Nobody had ever done church like this before. What they did know, however, was enough to keep them going and enough to sacrifice an easy road for their cause—"Helping people take their next step toward Christ . . . together." The Grangers started their church in their living room with ten people and twenty-five years later, Granger Community Church has attendees in the US, India, Singapore, the Philippines, Canada, and the UK ("Who We Are").

Granger is one church with many locations—from five thousand people at the Granger campus to twenty people at a prison reentry center to four hundred people at the RV Hall of Fame in Elkhart to one hundred people at Monroe Circle Community Center and more than fifteen hundred people gathering weekly online from all over the world ("Who We Are").

This church does a great job with leveraging social media. Their desire is to use their resources not only to reach people with the gospel but also to help other church leaders around the globe. One way they do this is through their WiredChurches.com network. In 2002, Granger started

WiredChurches as a resource and training arm of the church to share what the church has learned with other churches around the globe.

Additionally, many of Granger's staffers have their own personal blogs where they share insights with church members and other ministry leaders. In fact, there are at least five Granger staff members whose blogs appear in my Google Reader. I can't say that about any other church.

The City
Zack Hubert, founder
www.onthecity.com

As the new pastor of technology at Mars Hill Church in Seattle, Zack Hubert set out to find a way to harness technology to serve the church. He found numerous options for church management, for helping administrators with things like budgets and attendance records, but there was nothing built specifically for helping the people of the church do the work of ministry.

While taking time away to pray for direction, the concept of The City came to Zack as he meditated on Jesus' words in Matthew 5:14, "You are the light of the world. A city on a hill cannot be hidden." Drawing on his experience as a systems architect for Amazon, he set out to create a group-centered social network that would be all about encouraging church movement by making it easier for people to become connected, build deeper community, and be empowered to serve each other, their neighbors, and the world with the love of Jesus. And so, The City was born, and as it has grown, so has the vision.

Even at this very moment, The City is helping people in hundreds of churches grow deeper in community and stay engaged in the kind of whole-life ministry that shines as a light in the darkness ("Vision," 2011). Churches can visit The City and join this very exciting social network, buy the software, and immediately engage others in Christ-centered community.

Potential Church
Troy Grambling, senior pastor
www.potentialchurch.com

Potential Church is another church that is using social media to build community and spread the message of the hope of Jesus Christ.

Troy Gramling is the lead pastor at Potential Church (formerly known as Flamingo Road Church) in Fort Lauderdale, Florida. Pastor Troy has led Potential Church to an average weekend attendance of 11,500 across six campuses, along with a pastor on the ground in Asia who will soon launch the seventh campus (five national, two international). In addition, in the last decade, Potential Church has partnered to plant fifteen local churches around the world.

A few of those unique worship experiences have been captured in such creative series as: ivescrewedup.com, MyNakedPastor.com, ivemissed .com, and TheGiftRevolution.com. Each of these series was rolled out through a marketing campaign, but the church did a great job leveraging social media to help the series gain traction.

I recall first hearing about (then) Flamingo Road Church during the "My Naked Pastor" series because of the tweets I saw about it, whether people were commenting on the series or linking me to a blog post about the series. The church also leverages the power of television, and through their media ministry, Pastor Troy has had the opportunity to influence thousands of people all across the state of Florida and the Caribbean.

Joe Wood, senior pastor and founder of Reverb Church, Colorado
www.reverbchurch.com
www.facebook.com/pastorjoewoodfans
www.appmii.com

I ran across Senior Pastor Joe Wood's Facebook profile recently and was literally shocked to see he had nearly five thousand friends on his personal profile and over two hundred fifty thousand likes on his fan page. I don't personally know Joe Wood, but after following the threads on his Facebook page, I am very impressed with his love for people and the messages that he communicates to those who follow him.

Joe Wood is the founder and senior pastor of Reverb Church in Colorado, and he is changing the impression of church for a lot of people. A quick visit to Reverb's website and you'll quickly find out that this church seeks to reach people who are far from God.

Pastor Joe says about himself, "It is my personal opinion that the average person's perception of church and Jesus are completely skewed because of the lifestyles of those who call themselves Christians (including myself). It is for that very reason that I do not consider myself a religious person. I personally dislike religion, but LOVE GOD!" ("Personal Interests").

I can honestly say that I've been blessed by subscribing to Pastor Joe's Facebook News Feed. He shares daily encouragement and inspiration. He is leveraging social media and the tools to provide hope and restoration to those who are hopeless and in need of Jesus Christ. I also found it interesting that Joe Wood is also the founder and creator behind APPMII, a mobile app development company, helping churches, organizations, and businesses build their brand through a mobile app.

Jacob's Well Church, Kansas City, Missouri
Tim Keel, primary teaching pastor
www.jacobswellchurch.org

A handful of people who wanted to build community in Kansas City launched Jacob's Well in 1998. Their website states,

> Our name reflects our dream and our mission. In the New Testament book of John, Jesus encounters a woman who is at the fringes of her culture, a woman with great hunger and great need. Jesus reaches out to her and invites her into his life and kingdom. In so doing she becomes a part of a new community. In the same way, Jacob's Well is striving to be a place—like the biblical Jacob's Well—where people who are searching can encounter God and find

a place in his kingdom and community and join him in his work in the world ("About Us").

Jacob's Well is a great example of how a church can build community online. Attenders can create an account and join the online community, quickly uploading a bio, blog feed, and even photos from Flickr. The thing that may set this site apart from others is that the content is grouped in one location. In one place you can read all of the posts from the online community, including staff and members of the church. You can view pictures and there is a discussion forum area where anyone can create a topic. The site even allows for classified ads where people can advertise their rooms for rent, their need for volunteers, or announce their garage sales.

People of the Second Chance, southern California
Mike Foster, executive director and founder
www.potsc.com

People of the Second Chance is a global community of activists, "imperfectionists," and second chancers committed to unleashing radical grace every day, in every moment, for everyone. Mike Foster, a co-founder of POTSC (as it's commonly referred to online), told me they use social media to communicate a message of grace and hope to a world that desperately needs a second chance. They often refer to themselves as "the Red Cross for failed and failing people and the AA for those addicted to judgment."

The People of the Second Chance website is really quite stunning. Spend some time on their site and notice how they are leveraging social media—using YouTube, Twitter, Facebook, and Flickr to share their message.

According to Foster, POTSC relies heavily on social media:

> Social media is our primary strategy for engaging people with our message. We rely on it almost exclusively. Social media and "shareability" is always a priority in everything we create and do. For example, we have a "visual" strategy for communicating POTSC values and messages. We do this because visuals are readily shared through social media outlets like Tumblr, Instagram, and Facebook. We work with very small budgets, so social media allows us to have high impact, reach, and influence at very low cost.

POTSC's mission is to challenge the common misconceptions about failure and success and stand with those who have hit rock bottom in their personal and professional lives. They are committed to helping people walk through the valley and offer the soul care they very much need.

Mike Foster explains, "Our process will allow individuals to move from being trapped in pain, loss, and despair into the freedom of a second chance. This pathway will radically alter the person's current trajectory and provide the tools necessary to develop a life of wholeness. Our process also provides insights and tools for organizations who are navigating a leadership failure."

People of the Second Chance has recently commissioned a comprehensive process and assessment that will aide individuals and organizations to thrive after a crisis. Using top professionals in the areas of science, psychology, and faith. Phase 1 of this tool released in January 2012.

GLOSSARY OF POPULAR SOCIAL MEDIA TERMS

API—*application programming interface.* Allows users to get a data feed directly into their own sites, providing continually updated, streaming data—text, images, video—for display. For example, Flickr's API might allow you to display photos from the site on your blog. When sites like Twitter and Facebook "open up" their APIs, it means that developers can build applications that build new functionality on top of the underlying service.

APP—Popularized in the general lexicon by the iPhone, an app is simply an application that performs a specific function on your computer or handheld device. Apps run the gamut from web browsers and games to specialized programs like digital recorders, online chat, or music players.

BLOG—An online journal that's updated on a regular basis with entries that appear in reverse chronological order. Blogs can be about any subject. They typically contain comments by other readers, links to other sites, and permalinks.

CREATIVE COMMONS—A not-for-profit organization and licensing system that offers creators the ability to fine-tune their copyright, spelling out the ways in which others may use their works.

CROWDSOURCING—Harnessing the skills and enthusiasm of those outside an organization who are prepared to volunteer their time contributing content or skills and solving problems.

DIGG—A popular social news site that lets people discover and share content from anywhere on the web. Users submit links and stories and the community votes them up or down and comments on them. Users can "digg" stories they like or "bury" others they don't.

DIRECT MESSAGE—A private message in one hundred forty characters sent to an individual through Twitter. The recipient must be following you before you can send a "DM" to them.

EMBEDDING—The act of adding code to a website so that a video or photo can be displayed while it's being hosted at another site. Many users now watch embedded YouTube videos or see Flickr photos on blogs rather than on the original site.

FEED—A web feed or RSS feed is a format that provides users with frequently updated content. Content distributors syndicate a web feed, enabling users to subscribe to a site's latest content. By using a newsreader to subscribe to a feed, you can read the latest posts or watch the newest videos on your computer or portable device on your own schedule.

#FF—This stands for #FollowFriday. Twitter users suggest to others who they should follow on Fridays by adding #FF to their tweet.

FLICKR—Founded by two entrepreneurs and purchased by Yahoo! in 2005, Flickr is the world's premier photo sharing and hosting site. Its members have uploaded more than three billion photos.

HASHTAG—A community-driven convention for adding additional context and metadata to your tweets. Similar to tags on Flickr, you add them in-line to your Twitter posts by prefixing a word with a hash symbol (or number sign). Twitter users often use a hashtag like #FollowFriday to aggregate, organize, and discover relevant posts.

LIFECASTING—An around-the-clock broadcast of events in a person's life through digital media. Typically, lifecasting is transmitted over the Internet and can involve wearable technology.

LIFESTREAMING—The practice of collecting an online user's disjointed online presence in one central location or site. Lifestreaming services bring photos, videos, bookmarks, microblog posts, and blog posts from a single user into one place using RSS. Friendfeed and Tumblr are examples of lifestreaming services.

MASHUPS—various. A music mashup is a combination of two or more songs, generally the vocals of one song overlaid on top of the melody of another. A video mashup is the result of combining two or more pieces of video, such as news footage with original commentary. A web mashup results when a programmer overlays information from a database or another source on top of an existing website, such as homes for sale taken from Craigslist plotted on a Google Map.

METADATA—Refers to information—including titles, descriptions, tags, and captions—that describes a media item such as a video, photo, or blog post. Some kinds of metadata can be captured automatically from the device without needing a human to enter it.

MICROBLOGGING—The act of broadcasting short messages to other subscribers of a web service. On Twitter entries are limited to one hundred forty characters, and applications like Plurk and Jaiku take a similar approach with sharing bite-size media. Probably a more apt term for this activity is "microsharing."

MOBLOG—A blog published directly to the web from a phone or other mobile device. Mobloggers may update their sites more frequently than other bloggers because they don't need to be at their computers to post.

MYSPACE—An online social network similar to Facebook. MySpace caters to artists and bands who enjoy the flexibility of creating an individual "look" for their page. As with Facebook, MySpace allows users to "friend" each other and create groups.

NEWSREADER—Sometimes called a feed reader, RSS reader, or news aggregator. These gather the news from multiple blogs or news sites via RSS feeds selected by the users, allowing them to access all their news from a single site or program. Popular examples include Google Reader, Netvibes, and Bloglines (all accessed through a web browser) and FeedDemon or NetNews-Wire (applications that run on one machine). For a directory of newsreaders, see Newsreaders.com.

OPENID—A single sign-on system that allows Internet users to log on to many different sites using a single digital identity, eliminating the need for a different user name and password for each site. You often find that a blog's comment section will identify you through your OpenID information.

OPEN SOURCE—In its strict sense, open source refers to software code that is free to build upon. But open source has taken on a broader meaning—such as open-source journalism and open-source politics—to refer to the practice of collaboration and free sharing of media and information to advance the public good. Well-known open-source projects include the Linux operating system, the Apache web server, and the Firefox web browser.

PERMALINK—The direct link to a blog entry. A blog contains multiple posts, and if you cite an entry you'll want to link directly to that post.

PLATFORM—The framework or content management system that runs software and presents content. WordPress, for example, is a service that serves as a platform for a community of blogs. In a larger context, the Internet is becoming a platform for applications and capabilities using cloud computing.

PODCAST—A digital file (usually audio but sometimes video) made available for download to a portable device or personal computer for later playback. A podcast also refers to the show that comprises several episodes. A podcast uses a feed that lets you subscribe to it so that when a new audio clip is published online, it arrives on your digital doorstep right away.

RSS (Really Simple Syndication)—Sometimes called web feeds, RSS is a web standard for the delivery of content such as blog entries, news stories, headlines, images, and video, enabling readers to stay current with favorite publications or producers without having to browse from site to site. Blogs, podcasts, and video blogs contain an RSS feed that lets users subscribe to content automatically and read or listen to the material on a computer or a portable device. Most people use an RSS reader, or news aggregator, to monitor updates.

SCREENCAST—A video that captures what takes place on a computer screen, usually accompanied by audio narration. A screencast is often created to explain how a website or piece of software works, but it can be any piece of explanatory video that strings together images or visual elements.

SEARCH ENGINE OPTIMIZATION (SEO)—The process of arranging your website to give it the best chance of appearing near the top of search engine rankings. As an Internet marketing strategy, SEO considers how search engines work and what people search for. Optimizing a website for SEO primarily involves editing its content, identifying high-traffic keywords and improving the site's layout and design.

SMS—Stands for Short Message Service, a system that allows the exchange of short text-based messages (texting) between mobile devices.

SOCIAL BOOKMARKING—A method by which users locate, store, organize, share, and manage bookmarks of web pages without being tied to a particular machine. Users store lists of Internet resources they find interesting and usually make these lists publicly accessible. Delicious is the best-known social bookmark site.

SOCIAL MEDIA OPTIMIZATION (SMO)—This is a set of practices for generating publicity through social media, online communities, and social networks. The focus is on driving traffic from sources other than search engines, though improved search ranking is also a benefit of successful SMO.

SOCIAL NETWORKING—The act of socializing in an online community. A typical social network such as Facebook, LinkedIn, MySpace, or Bebo allows you to create a profile, add friends, communicate with other members, and add your own media.

STREAMING MEDIA—Unlike downloadable podcasts or video, streaming media refers to video or audio that can be watched or listened to online but not stored permanently. Streamed audio is often called webcasting. Traditional media companies like to stream their programs so that they can't be distributed freely onto file-sharing networks.

TAG CLOUD—A visual representation of the popularity of the tags or descriptions that people are using on a blog or website. Popular tags are often shown in a large type and less popular tags in smaller type.

TAGS—Keywords added to a blog post, photo, or video to help users find related topics or media, either through browsing on the site or as a term to make your entry more relevant to search engines.

TERMS OF SERVICE (TOS)—The legal basis upon which you agree to use someone else's property such as a website, video hosting site, software, or other digital media. Check the TOS before agreeing to concede your rights to the site owners who may claim ownership over your content.

TROLL—Internet slang for someone who posts controversial, inflammatory, irrelevant, or off-topic messages in an online community, such as an online discussion forum or chat room, with the primary intent of provoking other users into an emotional response or to generally disrupt normal on-topic discussion.

TWEET—A post on Twitter, a real-time social messaging system. While all agree on the usage of the word "tweet" as a noun, people disagree on whether you "tweet" or "Twitter" as a verb. "RT" stands for retweet: users add "RT" in a tweet if they are reposting something from another user.

TWEETUP—An organized or impromptu gathering of people who use Twitter. Users often include a hashtag, such as #tweetup, when publicizing a local tweetup.

TWITTER—A popular social network that lets members post updates of no more than one hundred forty characters. People have begun using Twitter in interesting ways to point to news stories, to raise funds for charity, and other unexpected uses.

TWITTERVERSE—Akin to blogs and the blogosphere, the Twitterverse is simply the universe of people who use Twitter and the conversations taking place within that sphere.

VIDEOBLOG—Also called a vlog, this is simply a blog that contains video entries. Some people call it video podcasting, vodcasting, or vlogging.

VIRTUAL WORLD—An online computer-simulated space like "Second Life" that mixes aspects of real life with fantasy elements. Typically, you can create a representation of yourself (an avatar) and socialize with other residents for free, though you can also buy currency (using real money) to purchase land and trade with other residents. Second Life is being used by some nonprofits and businesses to run discussions, virtual events, and fundraising.

WEB ANALYTICS—The measurement, collection, analysis, and reporting of Internet data for the purpose of understanding who your visitors are and optimizing your website.

WEB CONFERENCING—Function used to conduct live meetings or presentations over the Internet. In a web conference, each participant sits at his or her own computer and is connected to other participants via the Internet. This occurs either through use of a downloaded application on each of the attendee's computers or on a web-based application where the attendees will simply enter a URL (website address) to enter the conference.

WEBINAR—A presentation, lecture, workshop, or seminar that is transmitted over the web. In general, participants register in advance and access the presentation in real time over the Internet and listen to the presenter either through computer speakers or a telephone connection. Webinars are generally one-way and can involve chat or polls. There are a large number of companies that offer webinar services.

WIDGET—Sometimes called a gadget, badge, or applet, a widget is a small block of content, typically displayed in a small box, with a specific purpose, such as providing weather forecasts or news, that is constantly updating itself (typically via RSS). Widgets make it easy to add dynamic content to your site or blog.

WI-FI (OR WIFI)—Stands for wireless fidelity, a simple system allowing enabled devices to connect to the Internet within short range of any access point without cables or adaptors.

WIKI—A collaborative website that can be directly edited by anyone with access to it. Small teams often find they can accomplish a task easier by creating a collaborative online workspace using wiki software such as pbworks, socialtext, or mediawiki.

WIKIPEDIA—A web-based, multi-language, free-content encyclopedia written collaboratively by volunteers. Sponsored by the nonprofit Wikimedia Foundation, it has editions in about two hundred different languages.

WORDPRESS—A popular open-source blog publishing application.

FOR FURTHER HELP

Websites and Resources

Blogging for Dummies—This book is available wherever books are sold and has everything you need to know from A to Z. You can also visit Dummies.com and search "blogging."

Christian-Church.AllTop.com—AllTop aggregates the feeds of the top one hundred blogs in almost every category known to man. Under the "Christian Church" category you'll find church leaders like you who are already blogging. This would be a great place to start reading.

ChurchMarketingSucks.com—A website developed by the Center for Church Communication to help churches not "suck" when it comes to their marketing.

Click-Finders.com—A search engine optimization company committed to helping churches and organizations get found on the Internet.

Feedburner.com—Flexible RSS (Real Simple Syndication) service to optimize your blog subscriptions.

Going Social website: www.goingsocialbook.net.

Google.com/analytics—Advanced software that helps you track your blog visitors.

OntheCity.org—The City is a social network hub and software company dedicated to helping churches build community around the world.

Pagemodo.com—Create a custom Facebook page for your business, ministry, or organization for free.

Problogger.com—This blog is dedicated to discussion of operating blogs. There are updates daily to the site, but you can feel free to peruse through the archives section for more.

ROAR.pro—ROAR is a company that helps churches and ministries by creating web apps for them. See chapter 12 for a highlight of their services.

ShortStack.com—A service that allows you to customize your Facebook page with contests, sweepstakes, videos, custom forms, and more.

Tentblogger.com—An exhaustive list of blogging platforms. If you aren't interested in a WordPress blog or others that were mentioned in this book, you might choose to head over to Tentblogger and see what others are available.

Videomaker.com/youtube—Videomaker has many useful guides. If you are serious about making videos with real quality, have a look at some of their guides, which range from lighting to audio advice.

YouTubeForChurches.com—A website developed to help churches learn more about how to leverage YouTube.

NOTES

1. Robert "Bob" Holmes is a great friend and the former news director for WMHK-FM in Columbia, South Carolina. He is currently the communications director for Columbia International University in Columbia, South Carolina.

2. Matt McKee, CEO of ROAR and a great friend, provides these thoughts about social media on page 5 in his eBook "Be Social."

3. To find this information go to https://adwords.google.com. It will require you to log in with your Google username and password. Once inside the site, select "Tools and Analysis" from the menu bar, and enter "church" for Grand Rapids, Michigan, in the search form.

SOURCES

@StickyJesus. "Got armor? it's time to advance online." Accessed April 20, 2012. http://stickyjesus.com/2010/11/got-armor-its-time-to-advance-online/.

"Aaron Durand saved his mom's bookstore with a Tweet." Last modified December 10, 2008. Accessed April 8, 2012. http://stories.twitter.com/en/aaron_durand.html.

Axton, Samuel. Mashable, "Nashville Flooding: Twitter and YouTube Tell the Story." Last modified May 2, 2010. Accessed April 7, 2012. http://mashable.com/2010/05/02/nashville-flooding-video-pics/.

Bailey, Brian, and Terry Storch. *The Blogging Church.* San Francisco: Jossey-Bass, 2007.

Brown, Robert McAfee. "ThinkExist.com." Accessed April 20, 2012. http://thinkexist.com/quotation/storytelling_is_the_most_powerful_way_to_put/341013.html.

"Chris Strouth tweeted '. . . I need a kidney' then got one." Last modified December 1, 2009. Accessed April 8, 2012. http://stories.twitter.com/en/chris_strouth.html.

"Daniel Morales reunites with his daughter after 11 years." Last modified February 24, 2011. Accessed April 8, 2012.

Digital Mom Blog, "Instagram Stats." Last modified January 4, 2012. Accessed April 8, 2012. http://www.digitalmomblog.com/blog/2012/01/04/instagram-stats/.

"Dr. Willy Mutunga opened the African courts to direct communication through Twitter." Last modified September 28, 2011. Accessed April 8, 2012. http://stories.twitter.com/en/willy_mutunga.html.

Filbrun, Joe. The City, "Technology Isn't the Goal." Last modified 2011. Accessed April 7, 2012. http://www.onthecity.org/blog/entry/technology -isnt-the-goal.

Fox, Michael. "Fox quote." Accessed April 20, 2012. http://www.schmoodia .com/fox-quote.

"Gained a voice." Last modified August 28, 2011. Accessed April 8, 2012. http://stories.twitter.com/en/roger_ebert.html.

Godin, Seth. "The rapid growth (and destruction) and growth of marketing." Last modified October 16, 2008. Accessed April 20, 2012. http://seth godin.typepad.com/seths_blog/2008/10/watching-market.html.

Granger Church, "Who We Are." Accessed April 8, 2012. http://gccwired.com/ whoweare.

Griffith, Wendy. CBN News, "Millions Plug into the 'Bible App Revolution.'" Last modified May 7, 2011. Accessed April 8, 2012. http://www.cbn.com/ cbnnews/healthscience/2011/May/Biblically-Engaged-A-Bible-App -Revolution/.

Jacob's Well Church, "About Us." Accessed April 8, 2012. http://www.jacobs wellchurch.org/about_us.

Li, Charlene, "Episode 99," Catalyst Podcast, compact disc, http://www .catalystspace.com/content/podcast/catalyst_podcast_episode_99/.

Mollencamp, Garrick. Wall Street Journal, "Americans Pledge Millions, but Cash Flow Takes Weeks." Last modified January 16, 2010. Accessed April

7, 2012. http://online.wsj.com/article/SB1000142405274870438160457
5005412610261000.html.

Murdoch, R. NewsCorp, "The Dawn of a New Age of Discovery: Media 2006."
Accessed April 20, 2012. http://www.newscorp.com/news/news_285
.html.

Naslund, Amber. "Social Media Today." Last modified January 3, 2010. Accessed June 7, 2012. http://socialmediatoday.com/index.php?q=SMC/
161834.

Northland Church, "The History of Northland, a Church Distributed." Last
modified 2012. Accessed April 8, 2012. http://www.northlandchurch.net/
articles/history.

"Okan Bayulgen and Akut saved two people trapped by the earthquake in
Turkey." Last modified October 23, 2011. Accessed April 8, 2012. http://
stories.twitter.com/en/okan_bayulgen.html.

Pastor Joe Wood, "Personal Interests." Accessed April 8, 2012. http://www
.facebook.com/pastorjoewoodfans/info.

Practical Social Media University, "Using YouTube, The Second Largest Search
Engine In the World, For Business." Last modified 2012. Accessed June 7,
2012. http://practicalsocialmedia.com/webinar/webinar-search-engine
-rankings-and-online-reputation/.

Qualman, Eric. "Over 50% of the World's Population is Under 30—Social Media on the Rise." Accessed April 20, 2012. http://www.socialnomics
.net/2010/04/13/over-50-of-the-worlds-population-is-under-30-social
-media-on-the-rise/.

_____. "Social Media Revolution." Last modified May 5, 2010. Accessed April 7, 2012. http://www.socialnomics.net/2010/05/05/social-media-revolution-2-refresh/.

Revehl, Rachel. USA Today, "Pastors are flocking to Facebook, Twitter." Last modified December 17, 2010. Accessed April 8, 2012. http://www.usatoday.com/news/religion/2010-12-17-facebookfaith17_ST_N.htm.

Schmoyer, Tim. Student Ministry Network, "A FREE missions trip for your youth group." Accessed April 20, 2012. http://www.studentministry.org/a-free-missions-trip-for-your-youth-group/.

Selders, Kevin. Relevant, "TwitChange Is Using Twitter for Good." Last modified 2011. Accessed April 8, 2012. http://www.relevantmagazine.com/god/mission/features/22962-twitchange-using-Twitter-for-good.

Stevens, Tim. *Pop Goes the Church*. Canby, IN: Power, 2010.

Stratten, Scott. "UnMarketing." Last modified April 15, 2012. Accessed June 11, 2012. http://www.unmarketing.com/.

The City, "The Vision." Last modified 2011. Accessed April 8, 2012. http://www.onthecity.org/whats-the-city/catch-the-vision/.

Voelz, John. "Vertizontal: Twitter Church." Accessed April 20, 2012. http://johnvoelzblog.blogspot.com/2008/06/twitter-church.html.

Webster, Tom. Edison Research, "The Social Habit 2011." Accessed April 20, 2012. http://www.edisonresearch.com/home/archives/2011/05/the_social_habit_2011.php.

WFC, "Join the Impact Movement." Accessed April 20, 2012. http://wfcimpact.com/.

YouTube, "Statistics." Accessed April 8, 2012. http://www.youtube.com/t/press_statistics.

ABOUT THE AUTHORS

Terrace Crawford is a nationally recognized speaker, a mentor to youth and youth workers, a social media consultant, a writer and editor for ChurchLeaders.com, and a chicken wing connoisseur . . . or at least that is what his Twitter bio says. Terrace connects daily with people around the world through social media. Here's how you can reach him:

www.terracecrawford.com

www.facebook.com/terracecrawfordofficial

www.Twitter.com/terracecrawford

Sean Cannell, who contributed the chapter on YouTube, is the director of Communications at The Church at South Las Vegas, and the co-founder of THiNK International and THiNK media TV. Sean has seen massive results using social media and specifically online video in a local church and nonprofit context. Sean's videos have reached around the world and have received a quarter of a million views in under two years. Sean is a writer, speaker, and trainer who helps organizations get their message out using traditional and new forms of media. For more information, visit seancannell.com.